PRISONER OF WAR

PRISONER

OF WAR

KURT E. B. MOLZAHN

Muhlenberg Press
Philadelphia

MUHLENBERG

DEDICATION

The story of my experiences during World War II, as told in this book, could not have been written without the actual help, advice, and wise counsel of my defender and friend

T. HENRY WALNUT

whose untiring efforts in my behalf and for my defense helped me to keep faith in God and my country. To him must go my deepest gratitude. I also feel it a sacred duty to remember gratefully my chief defender, the late Francis Fisher Kane, former United States Attorney, and the attorneys of Hartford, Connecticut, James W. Carpenter and Cyril Coleman. Gratefully I remember also the many faithful friends—within the church realm and outside of it—who stood by me and my family in those darkened days.

My deepest feelings of gratitude embrace my beloved wife and good companion in good and evil days, Nina, whose love, encouragement and never-failing faith have been my inspiration through all the years of ministry in America and have been my greatest help on my weary road during the trying years.

May my experiences also bear witness to God's friendly guidance and providence while testing our faith severely in order that we may be able to serve Him anew in His Kingdom.

K. E. B. M.

CONTENTS

INTRODUCTION

There is a passage in Paul's Letter to the Romans which is a comfort in time of trouble. It is verse 28 in chapter 8, and reads in the King James version,

> And we know that all things work together for good to them that love God, to them who are the called according to his purpose.

It is a minister's habit to speak to a text, though the story I have to tell is far from a sermon. I went to prison for a term that seemed—when I entered—forever. The manner in which I was sent and my life while I was there has haunted me to a point where, like the Ancient Mariner, I feel compelled to tell it. The tale is not melodrama of which moving pictures are made. The greatest suffering prisoners endure cannot be caught on a film, but it is nevertheless poignant. A man is as he thinks; he is a creature of his own imagination, and that part of him which one can't see is sensitive and receives brutal treatment even in the best-ordered jails. I don't suggest it can or should be otherwise. I will leave that to penologists.

It may be said that the feelings of a minister can be hurt more than those of the others, who are hardened creatures, merely numbered robots in prison suits, but I never met any robots. They were all people, and when you came to know them and their stories you knew that their suffering was real and that they had need for some such text as I have cited—a faith in a Being whose wisdom and guidance could be relied upon. There was more searching for help like this than one might expect.

A minister is at a disadvantage in a prison, but he should have the advantage of a faith in God and his purpose. My faith may have faltered many times but it could be recovered.

In order to understand the feelings of a prisoner, you must know about him, so I shall begin by telling who and what I am.

1.

'LUCKY KURT'

My family and forebears belonged to the Western Christian Church, specifically the branch known as Evangelical Lutheran in Germany, which for generations provided my people with the form of their faith. I was brought up in the church and its teachings. My mother, who was devout in her worship, saw to that, but I may add she had no difficulty in eliciting my interest. I knew she wanted her oldest son to enter the ministry, but I also knew that I never contemplated any other calling. Before I was fourteen I had developed my thought into a plan to serve the church in America. Perhaps my mother willed that also, although I considered it my own idea of which she approved. She could not foresee the price I was to pay, but I doubt if that would have deterred her. She had a faith that was quiet and profound, and she expected great purposes to call for great sacrifices.

There were to be more obstacles in the way of my plan than anyone expected. I completed my early education and prepared for the Theological Seminary at Kropp, which emphasized the training of Lutheran ministers for the foreign field, especially the United States. It was the church in this country that provided the seminary with its principal means of support.

It was 1912, when to my generation the world still seemed a secure and predictable place in which to live. There were individual ups and downs—of that we were fully aware. Our grandfather had provided a fund for the education of his

1

three grandsons, but it had disappeared mysteriously in the vicissitudes of the business world, so the management of our household called for the greatest prudence. But the form of society itself was set in a mold. It seemed as if it must have been so always, and would always remain. We accepted it as natural and proper. There was a confidence in the stability of the future that came with the conviction that the common interests of all were so intertwined in world commerce that great wars were unthinkable. I accepted that belief without question.

At seventeen we are all great egotists. Our minds center on the meaning of our own lives. I concentrated on my daily grind of study and my own progress. My timetable showed a certain number of years for study followed by the great adventure of a new land, new people, and new opportunities. I was not escaping from any sort of economic oppression, for Germany at that time offered many opportunities. It had grown lusty under the new empire. It was busy. It seemed solid and secure. It was strong and had the pride of strength. At the top was the pomp and glory which has always impressed the imagination of man. It was a country to be proud of. It was my heritage, and I accepted it with pride.

I was nineteen and on vacation from preparatory school when the war came in 1914. The conscription age had at once been reduced to eighteen. There was a family conference. I became a dragoon in the first regiment of the guards, whose honorary commander had been Queen Victoria of Great Britain and Ireland. We wore her insignia on our uniforms.

The guards were a famous cavalry regiment. I had grown up with horses and loved them. Moreover, war looked more glorious to dragoons than to infantrymen. No one then comprehended the new meaning of war. We began with a full measure of glory. The Kaiser reviewed his troops. The dragoons rode before him in their splendid uniforms, their steel helmets topped with flaming plumes, their erect lances with flying pennants moving like a forest, and the beat of unnumbered hoofs enveloping the rider in a rhythmic confusion of sound that was intoxicating. I was young. I had a proud horse between my knees, a commanding grip upon the bridle reins. All around me were fine, manly fellows. I was bound to them and they to me in a common cause. It was the Fatherland we must never disgrace, and the regiment with its motto, *Nunquam Retrosum*. Never Retreat.

Our regiment met its pledges to the full. It was shot to pieces and reformed more than once. Few of its original members survived and most of those who did came out with scars that spoke of the miraculous things that happen when death comes so close and yet passes by.

For four years I was on the Russian front and like to think that I did my duty as a man should. Through two winters we had to fight the cold as much as our human enemies. It penetrated everywhere and never relented. It took its toll. The wonder lies in the number that survived.

I was in the Ukraine in 1918 when the war ended and the German armies withdrew. As an officer, I started my small command on the trek back to Germany. The Communists moved in as we moved out. It took us a month or more to go fifteen hundred miles, part on foot, part by rail. The last stretch by rail ended at Allenstein in East Prussia. We expected an appreciative welcome, but were met at the station by members of the Labor and Soldiers Counsel, who had spent the war behind the lines. When they demanded that we give up our arms, I refused and was put under arrest, but was promptly released by my men. It was an unhappy homecoming. Finally we reached Berlin and found it no happier. Red banners draped the Brandenburger Tor, small arms and machine guns were spitting all along Unter den Linden. I met my mother and some relatives there. I was in broken health; they sent me to relatives in the country to recuperate in more familiar surroundings.

In May, 1919, the preparatory school I had attended before the war managed to reopen, so I returned to my studies. Two years later I graduated and moved on to Kropp for three years of grueling training.

In Schleswig, only a few miles from Kropp, I met my wife. I recall that ancient Nordic city with affection; young people, fortunately, cannot be expected to spend much time bemoaning past catastrophes—today and tomorrow are theirs. We had a happy time.

Nina's father, a former imperial judge serving as counselor to the head of Schleswig-Holstein's Department of Church and School, was introduced to me by my English tutor, a maiden lady of ripe years, who was related to the counselor's wife. She cautioned me against the counselor's two beautiful daughters, but, as an old soldier, I brashly claimed immunity in such matters. Wearing my only appropriate suit, the uniform of the guard, I hitched my horse to a dogcart and arrived at the centuries-old government mansion in Schleswig where the counselor lived.

There were no beautiful young ladies at all—only a photograph on the counselor's desk. His older daughter, he told me, was presently attending horticultural college near Berlin. The photograph fascinated me—romantically unreal as it may seem—and though I was not to meet its subject for many months, I became an accepted friend of the family and heard much of her, all of which I stored in my memory. She was young, eighteen, and popular, known for her high spirits and laughter; I was a twenty-seven-year-old war veteran, feeling somewhat drab and solemn in the company of Nina's young friends who gathered at the house. They looked forward to her return for the Christmas holidays enthusiastically, especially one young naval officer whose obvious interest in Nina and cheerful familiarity with the family disturbed me greatly.

For, at least in my imagination, she was mine. I can assure those who doubt "love at first sight" that such things do happen—even when the first sight happens to be a photograph. But, when I pictured her surrounded by her friends and youthful suitors, I knew I could hardly expect to take her away from such gaiety and comfort to share the life I anticipated for myself. When the Christmas holidays did arrive, warned by my English tutor that I would not be especially welcome in the intimacy of homecoming at the counselor's house, I spent the holidays with my own family hundreds of miles away and did not return to Schleswig until Nina was safely back at school.

Three months later I met her face to face. The spring vacation was just beginning and I was invited to the counselor's for a formal afternoon coffee and dinner. Nina would be home. It was the moment I had waited for and feared. I resolved to face it. Correctly attired in cutaway coat—Germany was in economic straits and was gasping for breath, but Schleswig society determinedly preserved all the traditional forms—I entered the house, presented my hostess with flowers, gave my courtliest bow, looked about and saw Nina. The picture came to life in beautiful colors. She seemed surprised when she met me. Later I learned she expected a badly crippled figure; Germany was full of war cripples.

Although I saw much of Nina during the next two weeks, having secured quarters in Schleswig and participating in its social life, I never could come close to her. She was always in the company of others. Distracted and frustrated, I joined a fellow student, Rupert, for a jaunt to the Island of Oland off the coast in the North Sea. It was the last week of vacation—I longed for solitude, the chance to think things over. It was no use. The peaceful island brought me no peace. We decided to return to school at Kropp, stopping off in Schleswig.

I had no intention of visiting the counselor's house, but we encountered him in the street, and he insisted we both spend the night at his home before going on to school. That evening I sat on one side of Nina, with Rupert on the other. They carried on a gay conversation in which I participated but little—my efforts to be cheerful were clumsy. The young naval officer arrived and invited Nina to a yachting party. She did not go and he stayed. The gay conversation continued. I wished I had gone straight on to Kropp.

We walked to the train the following evening—the English tutor, the counselor, and Rupert ahead, Nina and myself following. I talked of my plans. They were something about which I could speak freely and, I thought, safely, but I found myself looking at her and saying, "*Gnädiges Fräulein,* my fondest wish is that you might join me in America. Will you?" She met my gaze squarely and said without hesitation, "I will." It was as simple as that. Maybe most great events in our lives happen with equal simplicity. We shook hands gravely as if we were sealing a pact. The train came in. Rupert and the tutor went up the car steps ahead of me. I reached the top and waved goodbye. Nina's face was turned up toward me. Then it all came clear. I shouted, "Rupert, look after the luggage. I am staying here. I am engaged." The tutor followed me down the steps. Rupert gazed after me, "Lucky Kurt, if you hadn't asked her, I would have." He was waving to us as the train pulled out.

Then came the scene in the station waiting room. In one corner I humbly apologized to the counselor for having spoken without first consulting him: I explained that my act was quite involuntary. In another corner, my tutor reproached Nina for having been so forward. The counselor heard me through and then in his most judical manner remarked that I was unquestionably guilty but he knew of no suitable penalty and added, "Let us go home at once and submit the matter to a higher court." Nina was submissive under the reproaches directed to her, but undaunted. Her mother received the news without manifesting any sense of outrage; in fact she seemed not in the least surprised. She took her daughter under her wing and together they disappeared. I was left alone with the counselor, who settled himself composedly in a chair, lit a cigar and watched me as I moved restlessly about the room; then he told me to sit down and said, "My son, since you seem resolved on setting up a household of your own, I will give you advice out of my experience. You must be the ruler of your household. You have noticed, no doubt, how completely I rule mine. Assert yourself at the beginning as I did." He handed me a small plaque, "Keep it always," he said, and I have. "The motto on it is the secret of your power." It read:

> Ich bin der Herr im Hause, und was meine
> Frau sagt, wird gemacht.

"I am the ruler of my household. What my wife orders shall be done." I looked at him. There was a twinkle in his eye. "Now I have given you the basic secret; I shall leave the rest to your own good judgment."

I have a great affection and admiration for him. He was a man of utter integrity, a just judge and a sound counselor. His vocation was the public service. The German system that trained men for such service and moved them up from place to place as they developed in capacity and understanding had much to commend it, but I suppose it would not be acceptable here.

The family gathered together again to celebrate the occasion and Nina appeared dressed all in white. There was a time when the others withdrew and we were alone. I can see now the arrangement of her hair and somewhere a red ribbon, all else sheer white. She seemed half-frightened and half-expectant. I could not touch her.

The formal announcement of our engagement, complete with large reception, was made in August, and thereafter we saw little of each other. Nina went back to Berlin, and I returned to Kropp for my last year of schooling, which was somehow suffused by a light that touched the dullest things with radiance. My letters to Nina were full of profound emotion.

Soon I was cramming for my final examination in Hebrew, Greek, Latin, dogmatics, philosophy, and church history. In a room in the rear of the counselor's residence I completed writing my fifty-thousand-word thesis in German and Latin— on "Luther's Attitude Toward Predestination as Disclosed by His *De Servo Arbitrio*." What I wrote is still in my memory (I shall spare you a recital), but that memory is haunted by the song of nightingales. Great numbers of them sang the night through in the park behind the house, and I often wrote far past midnight. I suspect that under such circumstances even Shelley would have been sated by their song.

2.

'HE IS A MAN ALSO'

In December, 1923, I graduated from the seminary and in January sailed for America to make a place for myself and to establish a home for my future wife.

There were only three of us America-bound from Kropp, the first since the war. One of the three became a learned professor in a Canadian college, another a highly respected pastor; neither was destined to meet any such startling catastrophe as later overtook me. My destination in America was Susquehanna University at Selinsgrove in the northeast part of Pennsylvania, which included a Lutheran theological seminary at the time. When I arrived I was housed in a student dormitory and gave instruction in the seminary in Hebrew, Greek, Latin, and church history; in the college I taught French and German. Thus I supported myself while receiving instruction in English and the history of the church in America.

I was shortly on pleasant terms with the president and teaching staff, but had some awkward moments with the students. They treated me with a familiarity and informality that would be unheard of in a German school, where student-teacher relations were slight and formal. I was addressed by one of several nicknames, and students drifted in and out of my dormitory room. I was "conned" into giving them advice with their studies, until a professor gravely informed me that I was interfering with the incomes of instructors who were paid for tutoring. I was invited into students' rooms, where pocket flasks of illegal liquor appeared in great numbers. My mother had been partially reconciled to my departure for the United States because that great country had abolished alcohol, to which she was firmly opposed; I never undeceived her on that score in my letters, but I did hint at the students' informal treatment of an ordained minister. I am sure she was convinced that the church in America was in a very bad way.

In the classroom, however, I was treated with proper respect, and found the students earnest and intent on acquiring an education. And I never was confronted by the least adverse reaction to my nationality. In fact, I was asked to speak on conditions in Germany. The students then voted to forego certain kinds of food that the savings from their self-denial might be applied to German relief.

The area around Selinsgrove has its share of Pennsylvania "Dutchmen," descended from some of the first German settlers in the American colonies. They have preserved many customs through the years, including their language, which is a strange mixture of German and English. Soon after my arrival at Selinsgrove, I was invited to conduct services at one of their churches. I delivered the sermon in my best German, and was surprised by the noncommittal faces of the congregation as I shook hands with them after the service. Finally one old graybeard decided to give me some fatherly advice: "Parr', du hascht dei sach gut gemacht; aber du kannscht noch mit gut deitsch schwaze." The words have a droll twist that I cannot translate; in effect, he told me that I gave a good sermon, but still had much to learn about speaking German.

In May I was ordained a minister in the American church. When college closed for summer vacation I was free to accept an invitation to teach summer school at a Lutheran parish school at Johnstown, an industrial city west of Selinsgrove in the Allegheny Mountains. The church for which I worked was large and thriving, but on the outskirts of town, in the suburb of Morrellville, was a less fortunate Lutheran church, slowly disintegrating because of the long illness and finally the death of its pastor.

I was invited to hold services there one Sunday—my congregation did not number more than twenty-five—and by the end of the summer was asked to stay as permanent pastor. It was a difficult decision. The church and the parsonage were located in a valley a few hundred feet from the main line of the Pennsylvania Railroad, an extremely well-traveled line. Not far away were the great mills of the Cambria Steel Company, whose tall stacks emitted heavy smoke pungent with sulphur. Often wind and atmospheric conditions co-operated to bring the smoke billowing down to envelop both church and parsonage. The buildings were run-down, and there seemed nothing substantial about the institution except its mortgage of fifteen thousand dollars.

Those who had built the church were mostly Germans from eastern and southern Europe, particularly Hungary. Their language was somewhat different from mine and changes of customs and family names had taken place, but still they held to their original church and knew their Bible in the language of Martin Luther. Even the older members spoke English more freely than I, and for the younger ones it was their native tongue. If I were to be their pastor, they would have to forgive my lapses in English, and I their oddities in German. Most of the men in the congregation worked in the town's steel mills or near-by coal mines. They were hard-fisted, hard-working, and some, perhaps, hard-drinking; but they were virile and straightforward. I had learned in the rough school of the army not to measure men by the niceties of their manners.

Still undecided, I returned to the University of Susquehanna for the fall term. I could continue at the university and probably be elected to the faculty; the surroundings would be most pleasant, but to be a professor required a change in my conception of my calling. There were other considerations: the salary offered at the University was one hundred dollars a month without housing; the salary of the church was the same, plus the parish house and a chance to set up my own household. These matters were debated in my letters to Nina and my family.

In October the question was decided and I took under my charge St. Paul's Lutheran Church. It was my first pastorate and I accepted its challenge with all the zeal and conviction of youth. Many of my parishioners lived in the hills surrounding the church, and it called for a strong pair of legs and a durable heart to call upon them. I had both. My sturdy physique was helpful, for I had no means of conveyance for the fifteen hundred calls I made in that first year. I was interested in the people with whom I had come to live; I wanted to know them and I wanted them to know me.

At my bachelor quarters in the parsonage, my only housekeeper was the church janitor, a mill worker by vocation, who helped around the house while I cooked most of my own meals. I thought everything was in order for the arrival of my fiancee in November, but when the women of the congregation learned I was to be married, they completely transformed the old parsonage. The janitor and I were utterly cowed.

Nina arrived in New York and we were married first in a civil ceremony, then in our own church with a minister friend of mine officiating. The women had taken care of all arrangements here, too, and the ceremony and festivities were attended by a great throng of people. I am sure my bride was much admired.

In my letters to Nina I must have been somewhat less than accurate in my descriptions of Morrellville, for she had pictured our suburb in terms of a Swiss mountain resort. In truth, I was enthusiastic about the place because of its people and the lusty life of an industrial town almost bursting at the seams. But to her the entire situation was strange and, I suspect, frightening. The scenery in late November was forbidding, to say the least: mine mouths showing as startling black gashes in the hillsides; beside them the culm piles upon which light fell and died; the coal tipples, huge skeletons, grim and black. There was a harsh beauty in that landscape, perhaps, but it was totally unlike anything Nina had seen before.

Then there was the railroad, slicing the town and interrupting its streets with grade crossings. The locomotives could be heard shrieking long before they reached town, especially at night. The shriek would grow in volume and intensity, until it seemed as if the monster uttering it were about to leap upon you in a final crescendo of sound. As you started upright to jump out of bed, the peak of the sound passed and started fading away. It was not difficult for me to become accustomed to the disturbance but my wife was never reconciled to it nor to the smoke from the mills which at times precipitated in the house as a fine sediment. I knew she was homesick—in a way that was devastating, like consumption. Even her sense of humor failed to save her. She tried. Life is never without its shadows and the shadow of my wife's homesickness hung over our household, but we carried on.

The congregation of the church grew rapidly. Former members had their interest rekindled and many new people joined. Not in a day, of course, but they did come and they constituted a devoted and generous band. Christmas day of 1925, at the end of the service, I was urged to come outside before taking off my robes. I found there a new Chevrolet sedan, a gift to me. It was the following year that the mortgage was paid off in full. We went on, remodeled and refurnished the church at a cost equal to the size of the mortgage. When the work was completed there were commemorative services. The church was filled for its rededication, pews, aisles, and gallery.

Life was full at St. Paul's. Sunday, naturally, was a busy day. During the week there were many meetings and the customary ministerial duties at marriages and funerals. I became confidant and advisor in a great number of intimate personal troubles which afflicted the families of my parish, and always there were the problems of the poor and their obvious needs. I made many acquaintances in the city outside the church membership. I discovered that public officials are cordial to a minister who appears to have the confidence of his congregation.

There was one man, however, who would have no part of me. I remember him vividly. Of course, there are always those who scoff at the church and go their own defiant ways, but sometimes even they grasp at the consolation of religion when faced with great trouble. This one grim-faced farmer, whose background was in our church, lived back in the hills with his second wife. He was a tall, powerful man, trousers invariably tucked into the tops of his high-laced boots, a large black whip in his hand. People avoided both him and his land; rumor had it that he was distilling illicit liquor.

I became involved in his affairs when his wife lay dying, reportedly shot accidentally by the man's ten-year-old son; few people believed the story, for the first wife also died in a strange accident. A coroner's jury had decided, however, that the heavy object that struck her on the head had fallen from the barnloft, and was not the handle of the black whip.

Even to the most hardened of us there is something incomprehensible in the passage from life to death, and our religion clothes it with mysticism. Thus the farmer allowed me to come when his second wife asked for the pastor. I knelt at her bedside; her husband remained outside. Before she died she opened her eyes and said in a low voice, "Parr! You came, God be praised." I prayed and her lips moved. She died. Outside the room I was met by the husband, saying, "Did the old bitch tell you where she hid the money?" I said nothing and left.

After the funeral services he came into the parsonage one day and I rose to meet him. We stood at arm's length. Suddenly he took two ten-dollar bills out of his pocket and tossed them at me; they fluttered to the floor. "Take your dirty money," he challenged, and I responded instinctively. I ordered him to pick up the money. He stood, silent. I seized his wrist and forced his hand to the floor. He picked up the bills and at my command followed me to the church and placed them in the offertory box. Then I curtly bade him goodbye.

I never had close contact with him again, but some news of his reaction drifted back to me. In a local speakeasy he had "goddamned that minister," but when someone agreed with his judgment he became even angrier and added, "But he is a man also."

By 1928 our little church had become such a vigorous institution that I was called upon more than once by fellow clergymen to explain its success. I was puzzled. Certainly I had never set out consciously to build a successful church. (If I had, I probably would have failed.) I only recall that I was eager to know my people. I had faith in them, which may have led them to have faith in me. I had faith in the importance of the work I was called to do among them. There was need of the church and the faith in God it symbolized. We gave ourselves to it jointly and it responded.

Early in 1929 I was invited to become pastor of St.

Michael's and Old Zion Evangelical Lutheran Church in Philadelphia. At the entrance to this church reads a sign, "This congregation was founded in 1742 by Henry M. Muhlenberg, patriarch of the Lutheran Churches of America." Located in one of the oldest sections of Philadelphia, the church faces Franklin Square from the west side.

Naturally, I was proud to be invited. Old Zion was one of the best-known churches in the area, not only for its history but also for its leading position among German-American churches, its rich endowment, and its central location. The scope of my work would be broadened there; clearly, it would mark an advancement in my calling. But, faced with the decision, I realized how many roots I had put down at St. Paul's. The little church seemed part of me; I felt that no matter where I might go, I would never meet with a more devoted congregation. Nevertheless, the decision was made and in June, 1929, we moved to Philadelphia.

When the church was first built, Franklin Square was surrounded on four sides by substantial residences and much of the congregation lived within walking distance. By the time I arrived, the east side of the Square had become part of the approach to the Delaware River Bridge, while the remaining three sides were taken over by businesses or cheap lodging houses. To the west of the church was the Chinese quarter of the city and what was known as the Tenderloin District of Philadelphia. The many sycamore-shaded benches in the square were always occupied in fair weather by inert and listless men. It seemed as though all those who were either unfit or too tired to swim in the sea we call society gathered in the square as in a sink. But the church, along with its four-story parsonage standing firmly erect beside it, held its own.

The congregation, which had long since moved to distant parts of the city, came on Sundays and lined the square with cars. The people gave me cordial support and I found myself embarked on a busy and gratifying life. There were the regular church services, the meetings of special groups, along with a weekday parish school which developed into a settlement school made up of children of many races and creeds. Weekday mornings were often spent in the church's sacristy interviewing a miscellaneous list of visitors. A charity fund was provided to be used at my discretion. With the sexton lining up my callers I could see fifteen or twenty in several hours. Some merely wanted certified copies of their baptismal or marriage records, but most wanted help. The depression years of the thirties had begun. Some callers wanted immediate relief, particularly the dejected frequenters of the Square, a few of whom had me marked for regular visitation. These I could help with money or an initialed card which would be honored at a near-by restaurant owned by a friend of mine. Other visitors wanted jobs. I had friends who were carrying on substantial businesses and they frequently helped me out. Many times I put three or four men into my car and drove them from one establishment to another until I had placed all that could be taken.

One wealthy member of the congregation donated new bells for the church specially cast in Apolda, Germany. Their arrival in Philadelphia caused much publicity, and the mayor of Philadelphia, whom I had come to know, delivered the dedicatory address. The audience, which filled a large part of the square, was estimated at twenty-five thousand. It seemed a significant episode to add to the history of the church.

Not long after my arrival I secured a half-hour in the early evening on a local radio station and delivered a weekly talk which had a substantial audience. I felt that I was helping deliver the message of the church to those who could not attend a service.

17

Our social life, too, was full. The old parsonage had a reputation for being hospitable, and I am sure it lost none of that reputation while we lived there. One time our guest might be an immigrant farm boy we had known in Schleswig, another time, German or Scandinavian stars of the opera appearing at the Academy of Music. We numbered sculptors and artists among our intimate friends. I never could understand how my wife managed it all with our limited staff, but she did it in such an effortless way that visitors always felt at ease and welcome.

My study was a spacious room on the second floor which accommodated my library of three thousand volumes in English, French, German, Latin, and Hebrew. I was called upon to speak at a variety of functions, including a celebration at the great John Wanamaker store and the meetings of an uncounted number of German societies. I delivered one of the sermons at the one hundredth anniversary of a Lutheran church in New York City, and St. Paul's in Morrellville invited me to return and deliver the sermon at the fiftieth anniversary of its founding.

Perhaps it may seem as if I have given undue importance to the "worldly" side of my calling, but I have never attempted to draw the line between that and its "spiritual" side. To my mind they have been one and the same. I suppose that every minister must decide on the emphasis to his own satisfaction.

Old Zion typified my conception of religion in society. If you walk across the Square from the east the church confronts you with its expansive brownstone front and its tall spire, securely based, pointing resolutely to the heavens. It fills the place with its presence. Beside it stands the parsonage, looking squarely at the world, firmly insistent upon carrying on where others are given over to hopelessness.

These two buildings seem to assert that the living should not despair and that there is hope on high for mankind.

3.

THE CAPTURED 'SPY'

For thirteen years I served as the pastor of Henry Muhlenberg's merged congregation. They were gratifying years, for my congregation grew steadily and showed its devotion to the church not only by its attendance but by the support it readily gave.

The decade of the thirties was an uneasy one. The phase of this unrest which especially touched me was the schism between the country of my adoption and that of my birth. The final year of the decade brought us upon the cataclysm of European war. We were separated from it by the Atlantic Ocean, but I was called upon almost at once to contribute to the support of families of German Lutherans living in Canada whose husbands and fathers were interned as alien enemies. The war was not so very far away after all.

A year later, Old Zion was the meeting place of the "General German Conference" of the United Lutheran Church of America. This group is but a small fraction of the whole church, distinguished by the fact that its members conduct services in German. Its congregations are widely scattered throughout the United States and Canada. I welcomed the delegates from near and far, and we listened to a pastor recently returned from Germany who told us to forego hatred whatever might come, for we were brothers in the church and the church should not harbor hatred. He spoke, too, of a world divided into armed camps and warned us that German-speaking people here in the United States might suffer isolation within, and hardship at the hands of, our own society. His warning was gravely received, especially by those present who had passed through the ordeal of the First World War in this country.

Another year went by. The spirit of war had grown in the United States. We hung on the verge of total participation. But even in a world that seemed bent on self-destruction, Old Zion carried on as usual. In November, 1941, we held the annual celebration of the coming of Henry Melchior Muhlenberg to America. It was our custom to invite to this annual event persons prominent in the life of the city, particularly those who were connected either by personal contact or family ties with the old church. I noted that a number of those who had once accepted with readiness now declined. I did not like to admit it, but my church was becoming an "untouchable" in its native land.

Within two weeks of our celebration war came at last, and the grim monster entered every household. The young men marched away, including many whom I had known in the church school and had confirmed in the church. It was an experience I had in common with other pastors, but I was also called upon to view at close hand another of the uglier features of war. "Alien enemies" (a term broad enough to include all natives of enemy countries who had not been naturalized) were seized and imprisoned. Many thousands of immigrants thereby became subject to peremptory arrest and confinement. In Philadelphia most of the aliens arrested were of German birth. Their number mounted rapidly into the hundreds, and about a dozen were taken out of my own congregation. Their frightened families turned to me for comfort and aid.

The immigration office at Gloucester, New Jersey, was a detention camp. I conducted religious services there upon invitation of the authorities. Many of those in my audience were acquaintances, and I could not help wondering why they had been considered dangerous. Of course, I made no inquiry, although at other times and places I heard the same question asked—no one seemed to know the answer.

Apparently informers were at work, and people walked in fear, drew into themselves, and talked as little as possible. Who knew what might be reported against them, or who might make the report? The day of the secret informer is an evil day for any society. The seizures seemed to strike unpredictably. In administering to those stricken I felt as if I were administering to the victims of a plague. It may seem strange, but it did not occur to me that I myself might be stricken.

In the middle of May, 1942, some six months after the war opened, the Ministerium of Pennsylvania, a body within the United Lutheran Church, met in Philadelphia. It represented congregations in New Jersey, Delaware, and Eastern Pennsylvania, including Old Zion. On the second day of the convention seven or eight hundred delegates came to our church where ordination services were held for men entering the ministry. On the whole, my life was fully occupied with the duties of my calling, many of which were performed in public view.

On May 25 I had the first indication that the Government of the United States was aware of my existence. I was served with a subpoena commanding me to appear before a federal grand jury in Hartford, Connecticut, the following morning. I was unfamiliar with such papers and sought advice as to its meaning. The explanation given me was that the Department of Justice was conducting an investigation and wished to have my testimony on some phase of it. I wondered of what possible value anything I could say might be, but I went.

It was not a happy experience. The grand jury, consisting

of about twenty men and women, met in a closed room. They treated me respectfully enough, but the young man who conducted the investigation, a special assistant to the Attorney General, questioned me as fiercely as if I were a criminal. He asked about every phase of my life, making it clear that I had been the subject of a careful investigation. I answered his questions as best I could. I had nothing to hide. But my answers apparently did not please him, for he concluded his interrogation by pointing a finger at me and shouting, "Isn't it true that you are the chief of the Gestapo in the United States?" I looked at him in amazement. The only reply I could give was, "Some questions are too absurd to deserve an answer."

It may be appreciated that I was troubled after my return to Philadelphia. On June 10, 1942, my gravest apprehensions were surpassed. About noon I was telephoned by a newspaper reporter who told me he had an Associated Press dispatch stating that the grand jury at Hartford had returned an indictment in which I had been named as a co-defendant with four others in a spy plot. I was almost speechless. I could only ask him not to publish the story at once. I was sure there had been a terrible mistake, one which would be promptly rectified. That was naïve, of course. The story was front-page material in the evening paper, and the morning papers gave it special coverage. One of them used a five-column spread to display the portraits of three of the plotters. My picture was included. The long story identified each of us, as well as two additional plotters not included in the picture gallery, and explained what we were charged with doing.

On that day, Thursday, June 11, I had little time to think about the charges, for the United States Marshal came to the parsonage with a warrant for my arrest. I was taken to the Marshal's office in the Federal Building where I waited until the United States Commissioner arrived. My appearance before him was brief. He held me under twenty-five thousand dollars bail for a further hearing the following Tuesday.

There was no way to secure that much bail so late in the afternoon, so toward evening I was loaded into a police van with five dope-peddlers and taken to Moyamensing Prison, an ancient and forbidding fortress that had stood for more than a century. I shall not relate my experiences of the next few days. They were like a horrid dream, which was over by Monday at noon when I reappeared before the Commissioner. There in the room were many members of my congregation to greet me. They had been busy raising thirty-eight thousand dollars in cash. Some of the poorer members had offered their life's savings; the Sunday school children had brought their savings boxes to church. The money was counted out up to twenty-five thousand dollars, much of it in one dollar bills, and I was released. It was a display of faith and loyalty to me which gave a sorely needed lift to my spirits.

The following day I was again before the Commissioner and was held to appear for trial in the United States Court for the District of Connecticut. The money already posted was accepted as bail and I was released.

Each move in the case was a signal for new stories in the press. I read them, of course. They had a baleful fascination for me. Before the first story was published I was asked for comment and was quoted as saying, "I am dumbfounded" and "My name was dragged into this and I don't know why." Subsequent stories appeared without comment from me. It was maddening, but what could I do about them? I might shout that I was innocent, but who would hear me? The papers spoke to millions.

One of the men whose portraits had appeared with mine in the news story of June 11 was a Count Anastase V. His name and his life history were new to me, but they were quite dramatic. He had been a titled Russian of the Czar's nobility and an officer in the Czar's army who had fled his native land when the Bolsheviki took over. Presumably he left his property behind him, for when he got to the United States he took a routine job in a big industrial plant. Later he married an American woman, the size of whose fortune excited awe in the press. He and his wife lived for a number of years in Europe, returned to this country about 1932, and took up residence on what was spoken of as a large estate in northern Connecticut. He shortly became involved in world politics as leader of the "All-Russian National Fascist Party," which was dedicated to the liberation of his native land from the Communists.

The second portrait was that of Wilhelm K., who had been national leader of the German-American Bund. In that capacity he achieved great notoriety and was vigorously reviled. His connection with Count V. was later made plain by a letter produced by the Government. It had been written to the Count shortly after the beginning of the German drive into Russia. The Bund leader wrote, in part:

The hour truly has struck for the final destruction of the Red Godless Scourge, through the liberating might of the Germany of Adolph Hitler. The hour has come for all those who are sufficiently young, capable and free of dependents here to go where they can effectively take part in the war to the death against the Soviet pestilence, for no such opportunity to liberate not only Russia from the blight, but all other nations from this threat, will come again in our time.

He prayed God that the "power of an awakened United States may also yet be lent" to the common cause.

My picture was the third in the gallery and under it was the inscription: "Reverend Kurt E. B. Molzahn, accused of running a spy post office in manse of Philadelphia Old Zion Church; innocent he says." I was not linked with any organization devoted to international politics, and it seemed to me that I was rather a drab figure compared with the other two. The story recited my part in the plot according to federal officers in this way: I maintained "A post office for a Nazi-Japanese spy ring"; I was a member of "the most important spy ring to be uncovered since the United States went to war"; I permitted "the use of my address [the parsonage] by the ring"; mail for K. and others in the conspiracy was sent there, and persons working with the ring went there to get in touch with others.

The others, according to the indictment, included Otto W., leader of the German-American Bund in Chicago, and Dr. Wolfgang E., a member of the Bund in El Paso, Texas. I knew neither of them.

I followed the development in the case as reported by the press. The Count appeared in court the same day the indictment was returned against him. He was accompanied by a lawyer from New York whose name was sufficiently famous to be vaguely familiar to me. The client pleaded "not guilty." The lawyer presented to the court a petition stating that his client was insane and asking that he be committed to an asylum. Action on the petition was deferred and the Count went to jail in default of twenty-five thousand dollars bail.

Otto W. happened to be in Hartford on June 10. He was arrested at once and taken into court where he pleaded "not guilty." He had no lawyer and could not furnish bail, so he too went to jail. Later a lawyer was assigned by the court to represent him and on June 19 he reappeared and changed his plea to "guilty," and was returned to jail; sentencing was deferred to await the outcome of the trial of his co-defendants. On that same day Dr. E., who had been brought in from

Texas, was taken before the court and entered a plea of "not guilty." He was without counsel and without bail, and was therefore committed to jail.

The following Monday, June 22, I entered the courtroom and was called upon to plead. Emphatically I said, "Not guilty." While I was there I was an interested observer of Count V.'s second appearance in court, with his wife and sister. I noticed the special assistant to the Attorney General conversing at length with the wife. He appeared to be most attentive. I saw the Count, a big, handsome, nattily dressed fellow, standing militarily erect at the bar of the court. He changed his plea from "not guilty" to "guilty," whereupon his lawyer, an impeccably dressed gentleman, addressed the court. His client was suffering from an unfortunate mental condition, he declared, the nature of which had been diagnosed by several psychiatrists of high repute, all of whom agreed he was afflicted by delusions of grandeur amounting to insanity. He submitted their reports and closed by expressing the hope that the court would take the defendant's unhappy condition into consideration in imposing sentence. Then the special assistant to the Attorney General arose to say that the Count was not the prime mover in the conspiracy and that the government raised no question as to the truth of the allegation of the defendant's insanity.

The judge, after a pause, addressed the defendant to the effect that in light of what had been established the sentence would be five years in an institution, where his psychotic condition might be treated, plus a fine of five thousand dollars. The proceeding took only a short time; there was no controversy. Everyone was very polite, and the Count walked out of the room with a deputy marshal at his shoulder. I never saw him again. His wife, I learned afterwards, paid the fine. With his money and his background, the Count had given dramatic coloring to the story of the spy plot, and his departure as an insane man would dim much of the luster of the case. At least the newspaper reporters seemed to feel that way, for they clustered about the special assistant buzzing questions. Afterwards I read that he assured them the Count was not the prime mover, but "Molzahn, he definitely was the leader."

Wilhelm K. made the next big story. It had a touch of the sensational, for he was arrested by the Mexican police on July 3 at a small seaport on the Gulf Coast, south of Vera Cruz, where he was living under an assumed name and busying himself with outfitting a twenty-six-foot fishing boat for a voyage across the Atlantic. Obviously, he was a man whose convictions could lead to taking hazardous risks. He was taken to the border, turned over to the United States authorities, and brought to Hartford where he pleaded "not guilty." Lacking bail money, he was committed to jail.

K. was a Philadelphian, the son of the organist of a Lutheran church, the pastor of which was a close friend of mine. I had heard about him and on several occasions had come across him at meetings of German societies, but I had not seen or talked to him since 1938—before he became headline material as national leader of the Bund.

On July 10 an additional paper was filed in the case by the prosecution which carried some interesting information. The indictment under which I stood accused with the other four defendants contained a list of what were called "overt acts"; one of these was that in August of 1941 I "made arrangements for a meeting between the defendants K. and E. in El Paso, Texas." My lawyers asked the court to direct the prosecutor to give more specific information, and the following details were provided: the time of the arrangements was on or about August 15, 1941, the place Philadelphia; "the persons with whom the defendant, Molzahn, made such arrangements were one Aleksy Pelypenko and other persons to your attorney unknown, and Wilhelm K., who acted by and through the said Aleksy Pelypenko in the making of such arrangements."

The curiosity of the press was excited by this news and the prosecutor was assailed with questions about Pelypenko. Where was he? What did he know about the case? The prosecutor was reported as being reticent, but apparently he gave enough hints to give rise to speculative stories that the whereabouts of the witness had to be concealed and that he had to be carefully guarded, for he was the man who knew the inside story of the plot and his testimony would confound the plotters. So Aleksy Pelypenko was hailed as the "mystery man."

On July 14 Dr. E. reappeared in court with his court-assigned attorney and this time pleaded guilty. Along with Otto W. he remained unsentenced pending the outcome of the trial of his co-defendants. A week later K. returned to the court; this time he too had an assigned attorney and he too pleaded guilty. He was quoted as saying, "I had to plead guilty as the trial would be nothing but a circus and I would be convicted anyway." He was returned to custody unsentenced to await the outcome of the trial, which had been fixed for the following week, Tuesday, July 28. Now there was no one to try but me.

The day before the trial the papers carried a final blast from the prosecution: the government was prepared with twenty-six witnesses to prove that Molzahn was the leader of a bizarre Nazi-Japanese spy plot.

4.

TRIAL FOR CONSPIRACY

My case was listed for trial on the scheduled date in the United States District Court for the District of Connecticut sitting at Hartford. It loomed large and incomprehensible, like a menacing shapeless creature of a dream. Less than two months before, I had been absorbed in the troubles and gratifications of my calling, and then this prosecution had appeared. It had taken over my life, it seemed to hold in its grasp everything I was and would be. I knew the trial was to be an ordeal, but I was sure I could endure it. It was to be of greater duration than I had anticipated, for it carried on from July 28 to August 21, and the record of the proceedings is voluminous. Any detailed description of it would be lengthy, sprawling, and confusing. I can only reduce it to its essence here, and I do so with the greater assurance since I hold a document issued to me many years after the event by order of the President of the United States that makes the trial appear less formidable and enables me to view it and to discuss it with detachment.

My case could properly be called a war case. True, it arose out of an occurrence set in the midsummer of 1941, some four or five months before the United States entered the war, but the prosecution was not begun until June of 1942, and it may be doubted that there would have been any prosecution if the war had not come. The trial opened in the eighth month after Pearl Harbor, at a time when there was battle action in many areas—in Russia, in the Mediterranean, in North Africa, in the North Atlantic, in the South Pacific. And near at hand U-boats were prowling along the Atlantic seacoast. The news from all areas was grim. It was received with grave concern.

On the home front there were almost daily stories datelined from many cities throughout the country, about the detection and arrest of persons accused of spying, sabotage, sedition, and even treason. These stories were acclaimed as exploits of the FBI and other governmental agencies in the stamping out of Hitler's Fifth Column. The arrests gave rise to many prosecutions, and at least two were in the process of trial when my own trial began. At that time I was too much taken up with my own case to pay close attention to the others. It was just as well, for the others all resulted in convictions.

I came to see myself as entering the courtroom to do battle with the United States of America, the society that staffed the court, the prosecutor's office, and the enforcement agencies, and filled the jury box as well. The combatants seemed grotesquely mismatched. I was somewhat relieved by the assurance of my attorneys that the law provided me with a shield of innocence which the government would have to pierce or beat down by means of evidence sufficient to prove beyond a reasonable doubt that I had done what I was charged with doing. The evidence it could present was restricted by many rules governing admissibility, the purpose of which was to see to it that the individual defendant was tried for the offense he was charged with committing, not for what he was or was suspected of being.

I was warned, however, that the rules were not self-opera-tive, that they had to be applied by men, and men varied in their reactions; that they had to be applied to facts, and facts were infinitely variable. Moreover, the application of the rules in a case such as mine would be influenced by the emotions evoked by the war, for at such times society becomes impatient with its self-imposed restraints. In addition, no one quite knew how the rules *should* be applied in a conspiracy case.

I have already indicated that the indictment charged me and the other four defendants with entering into a conspiracy to transmit to Germany and Japan information relating to the national defense. The transmittal of such information by any person to any foreign country with intent to injure the United States and aid the foreign country is made a grave offense by one of the two sections of what are known as the Peace Time provisions of the Espionage Act. The other section makes the conspiring by two or more persons to effect such a transmittal an offense of equal gravity. The conspiring becomes a complete crime when any one or more of the persons who are parties to it does an act to effect the object of the conspiracy; it is not necessary that this act be criminal or that the offense of transmittal be committed. The conspiracy may stop short of fulfilment, but the offense will remain as an intention at one time existing in the minds of the conspirators.

The evidence of such a conspiracy may consist of a recital of words exchanged between two or more persons which indicate that their minds have met in agreement upon the unlawful purpose, and a person not party to the words or the agreement may be held to have joined the conspiracy if the evidence offered shows that he acquired knowledge of it and willfully did an act to help it along. Knowledge and the willful act must combine; neither is sufficient of itself.

I had some difficulty in grasping this concept of a crime. I was unfamiliar with it. I had thought of a crime as an act done in violation of law. Here was something predominantly mental. The inquiry concerning it would be directed to criminal thoughts rather than deeds. The story of my trial should illustrate how such an inquiry is conducted.

On that fateful July morning I was not viewing my situation or my trial with detachment. I felt I was being swept along by hostile forces I did not understand, that I was going into combat with an enemy whose shape I did not clearly see but whose threats and accusations had assailed me for nearly two months.

No one seemed interested in me as I walked along the street flanked by my two lawyers, but when we left the elevator on the second floor of the Federal Courthouse, we noticed a number of people in the corridor, just idling about. They appeared to identify me at once, but merely stared and whispered. As we entered the courtroom, I noticed that the half of the room to my right, reserved for the public, was crowded. Every seat was taken, and many people were standing in the center aisle. Those in the corridor must have been the late arrivals who were denied admission. I was conscious of becoming the center of whispered attention. Shortly thereafter I was in the seat at the defense table that I was to occupy throughout the trial.

Our table was in front of the jury box, which was set along the inner wall. I faced the jury and day after day stared into twelve inscrutable faces and was scrutinized in return by twelve pairs of eyes. There were times when the thought occurred to me that we, the jury and myself, were the chief figures in the drama that was being unfolded. I was the reason for it, and the show was being enacted for the benefit of the jury. Yet we were the silent ones. It was my role to sit mute and impassive, and they did the same. There came a time when I broke my silence, but my speaking part was relatively small. They remained imperturbable to the last.

The audience came to watch the show. It came persistently day after day, though I failed to see much drama in the performance. August had many hot days when the tall windows were open to the full, but the breeze that entered did little to temper the heat, so we sweltered. The air was heavy with the odor of steaming humanity. There were times when the breeze carried the rumble and roar of trains passing near by, which blotted out voices in the courtroom. We had physical discomforts to endure as well as mental ones, but still the people came.

Back of me was the table for the prosecution. I could glance at it over my shoulder. There sat the young prosecutor with his aides and several FBI agents. I sensed in him a ruthless will to win, and in all of them the eagerness of the chase. I noticed how they looked at me, and I felt that I was the evil quarry they were bent on bringing down.

Between our table and the door was the one reserved for the newspaper men. It was well occupied. A representative of the Associated Press was a regular attendant, as was the representative of the local press, and there were reporters specially assigned by Philadelphia and New York papers. They sat there, sometimes nonchalant, sometimes disdainful, sometimes alert. I could envy their nonchalance. The whole performance was to them nothing but a job. At times I thought it a tough one, for I wondered how they were going to make a story out of the day's proceedings. They always made a story, and I always looked at it, although the looking made me unhappy and sometimes bitter.

But I have been anticipating too much. When I first took my seat, the jury box was empty. The selection of the jury took a day and a half, for each juror was the subject of careful deliberation in which an effort was made to weigh the unweighables of possible prejudice. At last the box was filled and two alternates chosen. They were sworn, and a brief recess was declared.

When we reconvened, the prosecutor arose to make his opening address. Instinctively I noted that he had some of the arts of an orator, for he stood poised until the courtroom stilled and centered its attention on him, then began, in a voice pitched to the room, to speak of the grave responsibility imposed on the jury in this most important case—a case in which the safety and welfare of the United States was involved—of the United States of America against "Kurt . . . Emil . . . Bruno . . . Molzahn." He uttered the four names in measured beats, emphasizing their German quality.

He went on to say that the defendant here was accused of conspiring with the other four men named in the indictment to transmit to Germany and Japan information relating to the national defense, and that I alone challenged the government's accusations. He identified each of the other four and gave their political connections and activities. Then he described in detail a meeting attended by three of them, namely, Count V., Dr. Otto W., and Gerhard Wilhelm K., held in a Chicago hotel in the latter part of July, 1941, at which the three agreed to collect information relating to the national defense which K. was to take with him upon leaving the country for transmittal to Germany and Japan.

Then he turned his attention to me. I was the pastor of a distinguished, worthy, and dignified Lutheran church. It was under cover of my calling and of my parsonage that I had carried on my nefarious part in the conspiracy. He described the part I played. I had permitted K. to use my parsonage as a return address for his mail; I gave to a person sent to me by K. the name and address of Dr. E., a co-conspirator, in El Paso, and I undertook to arrange for the securing of a certain false passport for K. to make it possible for him to get out of the country.

Then he added something that brought an audible murmur from the courtroom. That the prosecution would show that "Kurt . . . Emil . . . Bruno . . . Molzahn" was in direct communication and association with the Gestapo. I had to exercise firm self-control to avoid joining in the murmur.

The prosecutor closed. The further preliminaries ended. There was a huddled conference at the prosecutor's table, and then the first witness was called. I will combine his testimony with that of the second witness, for both were strangers and both knew the Count but not me. One was a newspaper man, the other the Count's brother-in-law. Both lived in northern Connecticut, not far from the Count's mansion. Both spoke of the Count's activities as leader of the Russian National Revolutionary Party. Between them they described his meetings with officers of the German-American Bund and with Japanese, the receptions he gave both groups on the terrace at the rear of his mansion, and his attendance at Bund meetings; they presented photographs of him and his possessions, as well as magazines with unfamiliar names that ran photographs of the Count with statements of the purposes of his party. They spoke of the Count's visits to the Far East to meet members of the party in Shanghai and Dairen. Finally, a pennant suspended from a standard was presented and was stood up against the wall by the windows; it bore the Party's symbol, a Swastika—a Russian Swastika, of course, but that was a distinction that passed unnoticed. When they were through, ample evidence had been put in the record of the nature of the Count's thinking—his "attitude of mind."

The next witness was the "mystery man." He was, according to the forecast, to reveal the innermost secrets of the conspirators. He appeared in the garb of a priest and gave his name as Aleksy Pelypenko. He testified in Russian through an interpreter. Under questioning he gave the story of his life, a bizarre story which I can only epitomize. He was born in the Ukraine, educated for the priesthood in the Orthodox Church, ordained about the time of the opening of the First World War, and was promptly inducted as a chaplain into the Czar's army.

After the Bolshevik Revolution, he became a parish priest in Poland and within a few years was taken into the Roman Catholic Church. In 1933 he was transferred to Munich, and in 1937 he was sent to Argentina as a pastor to the Ukrainian colony there.

In addition to being a priest, he was a patriot, dedicated to the salvation of his native land from the Communist yoke. He looked to the might of German arms to accomplish that purpose, and made contact with the German embassy in Buenos Aires, to which he gave confidential information of an undisclosed nature. Later, when he lost faith in German promises, he turned to the English and American embassies and gave them confidential information—without, however, breaking off his contact with the German embassy.

Early in 1941 he was asked by the American embassy to go to the United States to work for the FBI. He secured leave of absence from the proper officials of his church and sailed for New York, arriving about the middle of March, 1941. He also carried with him what he called credentials from the Germany embassy and instructions from it to propagandize for the German cause among Ukrainian-Americans. He reported to the church authorities in the United States, but neither to them nor to his superior in Buenos Aires did he reveal the purpose of his visit. He considered that his business.

He was received by the FBI, put on the payroll, and given an expense account. Whether he was paid anything in addition was never made clear. In April he was in Chicago where, through some fellow Ukrainians, he was introduced to Dr. Otto W., with whom he established close relations, for the doctor accepted him as one dedicated to the fight against

36

Communism. In May he traveled about the country and had interviews with a number of people. In July he was again in Chicago and on the 26th of that month was invited by Dr. W. to go to a hotel to meet with K. and Count V. At that meeting, he testified, he heard the three talk of gathering information concerning our national defense for delivery to K., who was to leave the country and transmit the information to Germany or Japan. In the course of the conversation reference was made to the possibility of securing a passport for K.

Shortly after this meeting, the priest was again in New York, and about the first of August he received at his hotel a letter from K. relative to securing a passport—the envelope contained two old passport pictures, and on its flap was written my name and address. When the priest received the letter, it was turned over to the FBI for photostating, and the priest then came to Philadelphia. He called at the parsonage. It was closed. He went next door to the church and found a man sitting in the church office writing, who told him that the pastor was on vacation and that his vacation address was not to be given to anyone; if the priest had something to deliver to the pastor, he might mail it to the parsonage. In his testimony the priest said that he nevertheless left two passport pictures with this man for delivery to the pastor.

Some days later a second letter was received from K. It contained three new passport pictures. The letter and envelope were photostated as before. The priest again came to Philadelphia. The parsonage was still closed. Two of these pictures were given to the same man in the office, with the same request as before. Efforts on my behalf to identify the man in the office resulted in discovering that the president of our church council remembered being at the office on an occasion when the priest appeared inquiring for me. The priest had left nothing with him.

The priest came a third time, on August 15, and on this

occasion he found me in my office. He conversed with me for ten or fifteen minutes. The following is a recital of the conversation as he told it, taken directly from the trial records:

Q. Tell us what was said by the defendant, Molzahn, at that time to you? *A.* That he received a letter from K. and did what he could.

Q. Did he say anything about pictures? *A.* I showed one letter from K. with his back address on it.

Q. Now what did he say when you showed him that envelope from K.? *A.* He tore this address off and told me to be careful with it.

Q. What did he say about K., if anything, right then? *A.* That K. was not very careful in this case. He said that K. was at his residence a few times. He is a good man, but he is not careful.

Q. Did he call him any particular name? *A.* He called him a dunce.

Q. He called K. a dunce? *A.* Because he wasn't careful.

Q. Did he say anything about these photographs that you had left? *A.* At that time there was no conversation.

Q. At that time? *A.* I just asked how I could communicate with K.

Q. What did he say? *A.* He gave me the address of Dr. E. in El Paso.

Q. The defendant, Wolfgang E.? *A.* Dr. E.

Q. Anyway, did you make a written note at that time of the address the defendant Molzahn gave you as the address of E. in El Paso? *A.* I tore a piece of paper off the desk there and I wrote the address down.

Q. Is this the note you made at that time (handing to the witness)? *A.* Yes, that is what I wrote. Up to this time I never heard of this name.

Q. You never heard of E. before? *A.* No.

Government Exhibit 20:

Prosecutor: May the records show that Exhibit 20 bears the legend "Dr. W. E., 111 N. Mesa Street, El Paso, Texas."

(Prosecutor handed government's exhibit to the jury.)

Q. Did you and Molzahn have any conversation about

how K. would get out of the country? *A*. I said that he expects to leave and Molzahn said, "Yes, I know."

Q. Was there any talk between you and Molzahn about what K. would take with him when he left the country? *A*. I stated that this business was very important, because he has with him important papers, and he said, "That I know."

Q. Did you have any further conversation with the defendant Molzahn about the photographs? *A*. I didn't speak to him, because other persons had been waiting for him and my talk with him was very short. In connection with this letter, Pastor Molzahn told me that in his correspondence with Baron Geinanth he had had an unfavorable experience with the Post Office, because of the back address.

Q. Did you ever at any time talk with the defendant Molzahn about these photographs that you left? *A*. No, I never spoke, I considered this business finished.

Not only was his business with me finished but three days later his connection with the FBI was terminated.

When I now reread what the priest said, I can feel again something of the resentment I then felt, which was not due solely to the fact that he testified against me. I thought it disgraceful that he should use the garb of his church as an aid to deceit, and I was revolted by his complacency in telling of the irreconcilable confidences he possessed and betrayed, as if that did credit to his cleverness and his mastery of intrigue. It seemed he must have deceived or lied to everyone with whom he dealt, and the conclusion is almost inescapable that he lied to the FBI. The prosecutor had asserted in his opening address to the jury that the evidence would show that the defendant, Molzahn, was to arrange for the securing of a certain false passport for K. Presumably there was something in the reports given by the priest to the FBI which supported this assertion, and yet when the prosecutor asked four times as to what was said about the passport pictures, the priest twice evaded an answer and twice denied that anything was said. So there was no evidence at all relating me to a passport.

I knew his version of the conversation was not true, and I can speculate as to why he did not say specifically that we talked of the conspiracy of Chicago and of the transmittal of information to Germany. Perhaps that was too crude for a master of intrigue, so by clever innuendo he raised the suspicion that I knew more than the conversation disclosed. Moreover, if his recital of the conversation is viewed against the background of facts disclosed by the record, the conversation appears more like an effort at entrapment than an honest attempt to find out what I knew of the conspiracy and what I was doing or prepared to do to help it along. The priest said he asked me how he could communicate with K., although he had seen K. in Chicago within three weeks of his visit to me, had received a letter from him postmarked Chicago within two weeks, and knew that K. was awaiting a reply. Moreover, the FBI knew that K. was in Chicago or in that area preparing for a national convention of the German-American Bund to be held in Milwaukee on Labor Day. So why should the priest have asked me something he already knew, and why should the answer he said I gave him have been given any significance other than to show my lack of knowledge? And yet he said he wrote Dr. E.'s name and address on a slip of paper at my desk. The slip was offered in evidence as if it added to his credibility, which it did not.

Also, the priest's further statements to the effect that I knew that K. expected to leave the country on important business and carrying important papers—these statements seem thoroughly unrealistic in face of the facts that K. did not go to Mexico until November, that there was no evidence he had important papers with him, and that he entered Mexico on a visitor's permit and was still there the following July.

I was called as a witness some two weeks after the priest had left the stand and passed out of my life. I denied specifically that I received a letter from K. or that I gave anyone the name and address of Dr. E., and I denied generally the priest's version of the conversation and gave my own, which was necessarily brief, for I had no detailed recollection of it. I recalled his visit and my wondering why he should be calling on me. I offered him a seat and listened while he complimented me on my wonderful and beautiful church and then entered upon a rambling discourse about the unhappy plight of his native land, the Ukraine, under Communist domination. He spoke in heavily accented German. Finally I stopped him by asking why, if he wanted something, he did not go to his own church. Whereupon he pulled a number of papers out of his cassock and showed me an envelope which he indicated contained a letter from K. On the flap of the envelope was inscribed my name and address. I reacted vigorously. I tore the flap off the envelope, arose from my chair, and terminated the interview, and as he left I told him as sternly as I could that if he saw Mr. K. he should tell him not to use my name in that way again.

I know that a learned judge in reviewing my case many months later suggested that this act of mine indicated a consciousness of guilt, but he did not understand. I had been under pressure for nearly ten years from two contending groups, each convinced of the eternal rightness of its own position, one insisting that I denounce from my pulpit the godless scourge of Communism, the other that I denounce the wickedness of Nazism. I was resolved that no utterance from my pulpit should do either. I would abide by the message of the church, which would survive this political schism. I was bitterly criticized by both sides and suspected by both. Mr. K. was the leader of the most radical group on one side, and I was both disturbed and angered at his use of my name. I showed my resentment by what I did to the offending inscription.

Whatever may be thought of my reaction, it certainly negated the prosecutor's assertion that I permitted K. to use my parsonage as a return address for his mail, and in this my version and the priest's are in accord.

When the next witness took the stand, I realized I was to hear the recital of another conversation. He was a man I had met on shipboard five years before. In July, 1937, I had received a cablegram telling me that my mother was critically ill at her home in Potsdam, a suburb of Berlin. It was important that I come at once. I had taken passage, tourist class, on the SS "Europa." The witness was also traveling tourist class, and we met after several days at sea. He was a learned man, the holder of several university degrees.

He testified that he had been a university professor in Germany and had spoken and written in opposition to the Nazi Party. In January of 1933 Hitler became chancellor of Germany, and in September of that year the professor was dismissed upon the ground that he was politically unreliable. He was not reinstated, and he came to the United States for permanent residence in May or June of 1938. When I met him, he was returning to Germany after a visit to a member of his family who resided in this country. As I recalled, he was somewhat stiff in his social contacts, but we got along amiably and made a sort of ritual out of meeting for a stroll on the deck twice a day, once before noon and once in the evening after dinner.

I could remember nothing significant in our conversations, but I heard him testify from the stand that he saw me wearing a Nazi emblem in the lapel of my coat, and that he heard me say I was a member of the party and was going directly to Berlin to have conversations with the "higher-ups" of the party. On the last day before arriving at port I gave him my card, on which I had written the name of my wife's brother-in-law and his title in German, *"Oberregierungsrat Polizei Prae-*

sidium, Altona," and I informed him that my brother-in-law was head of the Gestapo in Altona, suggesting that the professor call upon him.

Here again I could merely deny that I wore a Nazi symbol, that I had said I was a member of the Nazi party, that I actually was one, that I had said my wife's brother-in-law was connected with the Gestapo, and that he was so connected. I could go somewhat further and suggest the unreasonableness of believing that a permanent resident of the United States (myself) could be a member of the Nazi party, and the equal unreasonableness of believing that my wife's brother-in-law, who had been educated as a jurist for the strictly nonpolitical civil service, should be a member of the Gestapo.

I speculated then, and I still do, about what had gone on in the professor's mind when he reconstructed the memory of those five-year-old conversations. It appeared from his testimony that he had volunteered to act as a witness some two weeks before the date fixed for the trial. Five or six weeks earlier the newspapers had carried the story of a Nazi spy plot in which I was included, so I must have appeared in that character when he put the conversations together. He obviously had no love for Nazis.

However that may be, it is clear that in 1937 the United States would have had no interest in any statement I might have made as to my membership in the Nazi party. It is also clear that even if my wife's brother-in-law had been connected with the Gestapo, that fact would not have constituted a bar to my maintaining normal relations with him or suggesting that a shipboard acquaintance pay him a visit. It did seem extraordinary that such a circumstance should be accepted as a sound basis for the sensational charge that I was in direct communication and association with the Gestapo.

The admissibility of this testimony was debated at the time of the trial. It was accepted as the government argued, "on the ground that it will tend to establish the intent of the defendant, his state of mind, his motives for the alleged participation in this conspiracy and his availability to be held in this conspiracy."

There was one more significant witness to be heard. I recognized him when he took the stand. He was an FBI agent who called upon me at the parsonage accompanied by two other agents on May 28, which was the day after my return from the unhappy appearance before the grand jury in Hartford. He and his associates were very polite, and he told me of their mission. An urgent call had been received from the Hartford office asking the Philadelphia office to make an immediate search of my parsonage. He was frank in saying they had come without a search warrant, and he asked if I would agree to a search. I agreed without hesitation. Would I sign a written form which was presented to me wherein I agreed to permit the search and the seizure of anything he chose to take, and to waive any right to protest? I signed the paper.

I then opened my letter files and gave the agents access to my sermons and radio talks. They removed a few letters, and were given complete freedom in searching the house from the attic to the cellar. They found little of interest in most of the rooms, but they were intrigued by a mass of printed matter stacked on shelves in a hall closet. They took a number of pamphlets and documents extolling the virtues of Hitler and the Third Reich which were clearly of a propaganda nature. A number of these items were offered in evidence. All of those, I believe, had come through the mail over a period of six or eight years prior to the war. The mails were flooded with such literature both for and against the Third Reich, and I was on many mailing lists.

The letters that were put in evidence related to matters of a private nature or to the concerns of my church and my parish school. They bore the date of 1940 or earlier years. None of them had any bearing on the alleged conspiracy, but the correspondents were German and were identified as agents of the Third Reich or its partisans.

The purpose of offering these items in evidence, as the government said, was "to show that this defendant was possessed with a state of mind and a motive and intent which would lend itself to implication in the conspiracy charged."

The government rested. The defense was to begin. What were we to defend against? There was no specific criminal act, the doing of which might be denied and my denial supported by witnesses. The issue was more elusive than that. The government's evidence had been directed to showing that I was an evil person whose thoughts were evil. I sensed that it had succeeded in giving that impression to the courtroom. I tried to convince myself that I was merely imagining something and that my imagination was making a coward of me, but I could not deny that the demonstrations of amusement and approval that at times arose from the audience all came in response to some quip or sally of the prosecution.

We offered character witnesses. Some twenty of them. They came to Hartford at no little inconvenience to testify in my behalf in an atmosphere that was not friendly. They were all respected citizens in their several communities, some with reputations far wider than local. I heard them say that I was a man devoted to my calling, a man of honor and integrity who would not stoop to deceit. They stood by me stoutly and made it clear that in their opinion I was not the kind of man who would participate in any such conspiracy as that alleged by the government. I am proud of what they said about me and humble in my appreciation of it.

I myself testified at considerable length. I have already indicated those portions of my testimony which related directly to specific matters in the prosecution's case. The great bulk of what I said related to a miscellany of facts and circumstances that appeared in a review of my whole life—my family, my associates, my friends, my church affairs, and what I had said on occasions throughout a period of many years. I was subjected to a grueling cross-examination, and when I left the stand my spirits were not high. I did not believe that either my character witnesses or myself had succeeded in changing the attitude of the courtroom.

There was little more. Some answers that I had given to questions asked in cross-examination opened the door for rebuttal. I shall refer to one item, for it was peculiarly revealing of the underlying issue, though far removed from the conspiracy. It came about in this way: there was a church supper in the Sunday school room in the fall of 1939. It was managed by a member of the church whom I shall call Mrs. L. She invited a friend of hers to attend, a Mrs. Y. Mrs. Y took the stand and testified that after the supper, when she was about to leave, she walked over to a corner of the room where there was a table with jellies and cakes upon it, and there she saw pushed against the wall a pennant suspended from a standard, and on the pennant was a swastika.

Mrs. L. was called by the defense. She testified that her friend had been mistaken, the symbol on the pennant was not a swastika but the symbol of the Lutheran church, the "Luther Rose."

The testimony of Mrs. L. was the last to be heard at my trial.

Counsel took over with their appeals to the jury. They were lengthy and no doubt eloquent. I remember that the chief prosecutor described the sufferings occasioned by the war in terms so moving that several of the women jurors sobbed quietly, and I heard him cry out, "This man can never be a citizen of the United States in his heart. Once the fluid of Nazism enters a man it puckers his soul; and this man is a Nazi."

5.

'GUILTY'

When I entered upon my trial I had faith. I knew I had done none of the things of which I had been accused and I felt a deep confidence that justice would discover the truth and I would be vindicated. When it became apparent that no one was going to say that I had done any of those things publicly charged against me, my faith seemed justified, but as the days rolled into weeks and the prosecutor carried on with his exuberant violence, emphasizing matters which seemed to have no bearing on the charges, I became confused. It seemed impossible to determine what the trial was all about; my confusion, together with the stifling heat, sapped my faith, and it could not be restored. I became haunted by a feeling of impending disaster.

When a jury goes out after its final instructions from the court, there is a dramatic pause full of intense feeling. Some of the friends who had stood by me throughout the trial undertook to reassure me. They were certain the verdict must be "not guilty," but I was steeling myself against the worst, and it came.

To those who have not suffered it, the shock of hearing oneself pronounced "guilty" comes like a dull heavy blow; thereafter, the consciousness of it holds you in an implacable grip. I had lived through four weeks in an unreal atmosphere, and I now seemed to move in a nightmare. I stood with my attorneys before the court as they asked leave to file a motion for a new trial. Since it would be several days before the motion could be argued, I heard them ask the court to release me on bond to be covered by the twenty-five thousand dollars already posted. The assistant to the Attorney General opposed this motion with great vigor, interjecting such sensational remarks as that there might be a submarine waiting along the coast to pick me up. To me the suggestion sounded utterly fantastic, but the court refused to accept bail and the marshal laid his hand on my shoulder and led me away. He permitted me to stop and kiss my wife goodbye. She gave one startled cry like a creature mortally wounded, then was still, and I was taken to his office.

I was held until the court had imposed sentence on the three conspirators who had pleaded guilty. They had been witnesses in the trial with full knowledge that their testimony would be weighed and considered in determining the degree of the sentence. K. was given fifteen years, E. seven, and W., who had testified for the government, five.

At last we were on the move. I was taken down in the elevator with the other three. As we went out of the courthouse to get to the marshal's automobile a crowd greeted us. Photographers snapped pictures, and a little girl ran up to me and said something which I did not fully understand. She pressed a note in my hand. I read it in the car. It said, "You are innocent. I know you are innocent. I shall pray for you."

The other men were taken in a separate car. I was alone with a guard and the driver, a deputy marshal, and we started off for the correctional institution at Danbury. My companions were courteous and seemed anxious to lift my spirits by conversation, but the terrible thing that gripped me would not let go for a moment. We stopped at a diner for something to eat, but I could swallow nothing. It was dark when we arrived at Danbury. The institution is a great rectangular structure with high walls surrounding its courtyard. I went through the ritual of stripping and putting on a prison garb—

just overalls and shirt and shoes. The overalls were too large, the shoes too small. I was a woebegone spectacle. The others had arrived before I did. We apparently were viewed as peculiarly dangerous. Danbury is not a maximum security jail, so arrangements had been made to place us at the end of a corridor closed off by a special steel gate behind which we were assigned individual cells. The steel door to my cell had a square window, divided into four quarters of heavy glass, placed in the middle about shoulder high. The door closed behind me. I was in a compartment about eight by five feet with furnishings consisting of a cot, a chair, a toilet, and a washstand. It had a barred window breast-high looking out into the courtyard of the jail. I stood there bewildered, conscious only of the stillness.

For better than four weeks I had been the subject of contending forces which had been hurrying me somewhere, and now this was my goal where everything stopped. I could not think clearly. I could just feel that something terrible was oppressing me. I walked back and forth, I stretched out on the cot, lost consciousness, and came back to my senses again. At times I could not tell whether I was asleep and having a nightmare or whether I was awake and living in one. The time was punctuated at two-hour intervals by the sound of the corridor door opening and by the footsteps of the guard who walked past my cell door and shot a beam of light through the window. I could feel the beam searching the room until it rested on me, and then it was gone. The metallic clang of that opening gate reverberated through the corridor and penetrated my consciousness even when I slept.

Toward morning I was chilled through. Damp cold crept into the cell. To add to my discomfort, my left ear developed an abscess from an old injury. Also, I seemed to have lost control over my vocal cords; when I tried to speak my voice came in an unnatural squeak. I wondered whether I was going mad. Fantastic thoughts chased each other through my mind and I had to get a grip on myself and pray for strength to endure. I kept trying to believe that this thing which had happened to me must be corrected. Surely our federal courts would not permit a verdict to stand where a man had committed no criminal act. I knew enough of the county courts in Philadelphia to realize their human frailties, but I thought the federal courts might function on a loftier plane, further removed from the cry of the mob, and I prayed that somehow justice would be done and this horrible state in which I lived would be terminated. For four days and four nights I waited. They seemed to melt all into one, and then I was given a safety razor and told to shave. My own clothes were returned to me, and I changed into them.

In the administrative office I was turned over by the prison guard to the deputy marshal who had brought me to Danbury. I was being taken to hear the decision of the judge on the motion in arrest of judgment entered by my lawyers. The deputy marshal greeted me cordially as if he was glad to see me again. We drove off together. He was a lighthearted sort of fellow who talked freely and at times with great vehemence and much gesticulation. I learned that he was born in Italy and that he came to the United States when he was little more than a baby. This much I remember, but most of his talk flowed past me without making an impression. My mind was busy wondering about my family, my friends, and my church, and speculating on the outcome of my appearance before the court. What would it be like? I was full of both hope and despair at the same time.

In the courtroom at Hartford, I saw my wife and her closest friend, who had stood by her faithfully through all of the proceedings. My lawyers too were there, along with the attorneys for the prosecution and a number of federal agents whom I had come to know. There were a scattering of court attachés,

50

members of the marshal's staff, newspaper men, and the general public. The proceedings did not take long. The court delivered a brief opinion disposing of my counsel's motion. I was told to stand up. My attorney made an appeal for me. The prosecutor demanded a maximum sentence of twenty years upon the ground that I was the leader of the conspiracy and a very dangerous man. The talk ceased. There was a pause and I looked into the face of the judge and heard him sentence me to ten years in the federal penitentiary. I could hardly credit what I heard. It stunned me—all I could think of was that I must bear myself like a man and take the blow without flinching.

The marshal led me away to his office where I was joined by my wife and her friend. My attorneys came in to speak to me and told me that they were already arranging to take an appeal and I must not give up all hope. That was the only message they could give me under the circumstances. Soon it was time to start again for Danbury. The marshal, who had treated me most humanely and not in the least as if he thought me a dangerous man, permitted my wife and her friend to accompany me in the car, which was again driven by the deputy. The two women tried to keep a conversation going, but it kept faltering, for, try as I would, the thing that oppressed me would not lift; besides, my voice was almost gone. We stopped at a restaurant outside of Danbury—called Old Heidelberg—rather an incongruous place for me to take my last meal outside of jail. The notion of Heidelberg as a delightful place is common in this country, thanks to Sigmund Romberg, and I myself as a young man had spent a summer there and enjoyed it immensely. I left my wife and her friend at the restaurant. I shall never forget how my wife said goodbye without flinching, although I knew that her heart was ready to break. Then the deputy drove me on; I was delivered over again to the captain of the guard and returned, in my nondescript garb, to the little steel box of a cell.

6.

SOLITARY CONFINEMENT

When I found myself again locked in, I felt a desperate need for movement, so I started pacing that eight feet from door to window and back again. My ill-fitting shoes troubled me till I kicked them off and walked in my stocking feet. My stealthy stride made me think of the big cats I had seen in the zoo weaving endlessly back and forth in their cages. How long I paced I have no idea. My mind was a jungle of thoughts, and the horrid thing that oppressed me was always there. At times I could forget what it was but I could not shake it off.

I cannot recall all my emotions and thoughts, but they covered a wide field. At one time I saw myself in the courtroom with mocking faces about me, the faces of the men who had done this thing to me. I was telling them who and what they were in bitter, blasphemous words in German and English, words that had lain unused, buried in my mind since the days of the mud and the cold on the Russian front, words that came from coal miners and steel workers, forged in the pit, hot with hate. They burst forth in my mind. My fists clenched so tightly that the fingers bled at the tips. They were gripping soft white throats.

Then it seemed as if someone touched me on the shoulder and spoke: "What are you doing? You must not go on this way. May God forgive you, turn back to the faith you preached—vengeance is the Lord's, wrath killeth the foolish man. You must carry your cross. Watch yourself. Your mind

52

will explode, explode like that Russian shell, the one that was not a dud. Remember how it filled the air with earth and stones and odds and ends of men's bodies and equipment? But you survived—a miracle. God had a purpose. Your trial was a slow fuse; control it, pinch it off before it reaches your brain. Listen to yourself. Soon you will be screaming like a madman."

I listened but could hear no sound, and I thought, *That is good. I must not let those fellows know.* Then I thought, *I must be sane, or I would not concern myself with the opinions of others. These fellows will be watching to see how a minister of the church of God acts. I shall act as a minister should. I shall act as a man should for I am a man also. . . . Who was it said that of me?* I tried to remember, but the place where I stored such things seemed to have been demolished. Suddenly, however, there *he* stood, picked out of the confusion, that tall grim fellow with his laced boots and his black whip. I could hear him say, "I hate all men, and I hate God for spawning them. What good is your faith to you now? Look what they have done to you." He was striding along with me as I paced. I was ready to agree with him. Men were shameful creatures, and God spawned them. But then I remembered; my will had fought his once before. I threw back my head. Yes, it was a challenge, it must be met. One must stand by his faith in God and man. Either that faith is built on sand and crumbles or it stands on a rock and outfaces the storm. So I answered him: "I am a messenger of the gospel, a messenger bringing good news. That is my mission among men. That shall be my mission so long as life shall last. Yes, you challenge me, and a man fights back if he is a man."

Under the goad my mood changed—my spirits became exalted. I felt that I could exhort the world and fill it with faith. I paced and paced, and words and thoughts came in a flood, pregnant and compelling words. I was a great preacher. No longer could I be content with messages of comfort and faith; now I should blast wickedness with the thunders of Jehovah and exalt the greatness of God. How long my sermon lasted I could not say. It flowed on and on. It came to a magnificant peroration, and then it seemed that I stepped down and found myself again with the walls making straight perpendicular lines of the four corners of the cell. I concentrated upon the lines, fascinated. They supported the ceiling. They were so slender, too slender to carry the weight. When you stared at them they seemed to vanish and leave the ceiling suspended in mid-air. It was about to fall. I paced feverishly, that horror suspended above my head. Now I wasn't alone. A wicked eye was watching me through the glass in the door. It burned itself into my back as I walked away from it, it was waiting maliciously for the moment when I should be crushed. I caught myself turning quickly to catch a glimpse of it, but then an equally baleful eye took its station at the opposite window—no matter which way I paced, I was watched. Soon it seemed to me that the walls were moving. They started to revolve, and the revolutions grew faster and faster, and the eyes mocked me; the walls were bowing stiffly toward me, the ceiling was descending. I tried to hold back the walls with my hands, but on they came. I was about to be crushed. I cried out in terror, "The walls, the walls." I was overcome with dizziness and crumpled to the floor. It was all over. I could do no more.

After a while my head cleared somewhat and I got to my knees beside the cot and held my head in my hands; presently I began to pray. I prayed a long time. When I lifted my head the cell was severely rigid as if scorning the idea that it had ever gone into its mad dance. My mind was so still, it was as if I did not exist as a creature of substance any more. My ego subsided, and at last I could lie down and give myself up to that numb unconsciousness through which I could hear the clang of the metal gate and sense when the tongue of light came through the opening in the door searching for me; it would flicker over me for a moment and was gone.

I came to myself as the early morning light was entering my window. I sat up and wondered where I was. At first my surroundings seemed part of a bad dream; then slowly the reality came back, and something like nausea enveloped me. I began to recall what had happened the night before and realized that I must have been close to madness. It would not do to let that happen again. Later I was to see men go mad, go "stir crazy," as prison jargon puts it. It would not do to think too much. My mind now seemed dulled and muffled—how lucky, I thought, nothing can hurt me much now. I paced my cell slowly. I thought God in his mercy had deadened my mind and my spirit.

When a steel tray was handed to me by the guard with my breakfast on it, I sat and ate for the first time since I had entered that place. When the guard returned, I asked if I might be permitted to go out into the prison yard; I was told that orders from Washington prohibited it. That was a shock. I had not realized how eagerly I longed for space and air and light—even the little a prison yard might provide. I had to swallow my disappointment and seek refuge in my semi-torpor. I asked if I might have a Bible and was refused. Orders again. There was no alternative except to pace the floor or sit in the one chair and watch the slanting ray of sunlight which came through my window move slowly from one side of the cell to the other and then at last retire, as though its curiosity had been satisfied.

Standing erect I could look out of the window into the yard where men were loitering singly or in groups of twos or threes.

I stood watching them until my feet ached. I was like a small boy confined to the house, his nose pressed against the glass, seeing his companions play outside. I longed to be out there where walls were at least more than an armspread away and the sun flooded the air with light. I singled out one man after the other and speculated on what brought him there and what he was saying to the others in a group. From my second-story window I was looking almost straight down on them, and they looked as if they were all two feet tall. A number of them were obviously Italians. Later I learned that they were interned merchant seamen whose ships had been caught at sea by Italy's sudden declaration of war and who had taken refuge in United States harbors against capture by the British. Some of them wore jaunty and colorful caps. I fitted them out conversationally in the few Italian words I knew. One in particular held my attention; he was taller than the rest with the easy grace and strength of a leopard in his movements. He was fascinating to watch. A red cap was set atilt on his thick black hair. I pictured him with a growth of beard and earrings, a knife in his teeth, glowering over the rail of a sailing ship, a perfect picture of a pirate in the storybooks.

When I could endure standing at the window no longer I sat on the chair and tried to restore my mind to order by running through significant dates in history, the books of the Bible, or verses that I once knew. I found it a great effort. Probing into my memory was like pushing against a dead weight. I wondered if my mind was subconsciously endeavoring to seal itself off against the past. I found a place on the door where the surface of the paint was soft enough to retain the impression of a thumbnail—there I made a cross mark, the doing of which on each day thereafter was gradually elaborated into a ceremony.

At last darkness came, and I could stretch myself on the

cot hoping to lose consciousness, although it merely meant exchanging the nightmare of reality for that of dreams. The days went by, melting one into the other without a joint, all presided over by one central thought: *I must tire myself out so that when I lie down I shall be ready for sleep, or else I will be defenseless against a horde of thoughts.*

Once I was called to the front office for an interview with my lawyers. I must have been a sorry spectacle. An appeal had been filed, and the record was being prepared. It was indefinite as to when the case would come up for argument and be decided, but in any event this decision could not be expected for many months.

One of my guards tried to get me to talk about the case. I was not interested, and after a few efforts he gave up. The trial seemed so unreal to me that I felt it must be related to someone else. Another guard, an Irishman, tried to cheer me up. I liked the sound of his voice. He surprised me once by pointing at the walls, putting his fingers to his lips and shaking his head. He was trying to tell me that my cell had ears in addition to its other idiosyncrasies. That caused me no concern, for I had nothing of interest to say. Later, when he knew me better, he talked quietly about some of the officers of the prison. He named those he thought were not to be trusted.

Two weeks must have elapsed before I was given a Bible, but when it came I took it eagerly. It offered a chance to become absorbed in the printed page and escape from myself. But that was not so simple, for I found it almost as difficult to concentrate upon the printed page as upon matters drawn out of my memory. I struggled with the Book of Job as the one most appropriate to my condition. But there were times when I read and reread certain passages without comprehending any of their meaning. My mind seemed to be slipping beyond my control.

It is not surprising that I welcomed distraction—even when it came in the form of an ordinary housefly. One suddenly appeared one day and focused his attention on certain particles of my latest meal. I can remember that the Book of Job remained opened and unnoticed while I kept perfectly still and, with the intensity of a scientist, watched every move of the little creature. At length, when it had eaten its fill, it flew away and left me with a feeling of loneliness. I still had enough poise to find my reaction amusing. The fly continued to return for meals. In a day or so a second appeared from nowhere, and then a third, and we four shared our meals together. If I finished before they did I could sit in absorbed contemplation of their every movement.

I thought of a story that had been read to me when I was a small boy, of a Russian who had incurred the disfavor of the Czar and was sent to Siberia to be lodged in a dungeon sunk in the ground like a well. His food was lowered down on a chain; to him there was neither day nor night. It was a perfect setting for madness. His salvation lay in finding three pins which had been left in his prison garb. He developed a game; sitting in the middle of his cell, he would throw the pins into the darkness and then search for them, crawling about on hands and knees, a shapeless hairy creature uttering ejaculations scarcely human and yet not those of a beast. His highly sensitive fingers would touch every part of the floor. Those pins were all he had. They were of greater worth to him than gold and jewels might be. What a tremendous gamble it was every time he threw them away and what a thrill when they were found! Never was there such a persistent gambler.

After eighteen years there was a new Czar and new voices at court, and the prisoner was released. He was still sane. Man's greatest gift is his imagination, but it may destroy its possessor like an infernal machine when it is locked within the darkness of solitude.

Not long after I began my comradeship with the three flies, the Irish guard brought me a second book, *The Life of Mary Queen of Scots* by Stefan Zweig. It was given me with the compliments of a fellow inmate, whom the guard briefly described as a moving-picture man who had held out on the government in his income tax return and was doing a year and a day. The portion of the book I remember tells the story of the queen while she was confined in the Tower of London awaiting execution. The biographer credits her with a verse written in Latin on the eve of her execution. I read it many times; it has clung to my memory.

> "O Domine Deus, speravi in te
> O care mi Jesu núnc libera me
> In dura catena, in misera poena desidera te
> Languendo, gemendo et genu flectendo
> Adoro, imploro, ut liberes me."

This was translated in the book:

> "O Lord, my God, I have hoped in Thee
> O dearest Jesus, set me free!
> Though hard the chains that fasten me
> And sore my lot, yet I long for Thee
> In languish, in groaning, I bend my knee
> Adoring, imploring, set me free!"

During my third week in the cell I was told that I might write to my wife. I knew that my letters would be censored, but I did not know until later that they were forwarded to Washington for examination and perhaps photostated, then returned to the prison to be mailed. The delay in delivery amounted to at least two weeks. My wife's letters to me were forwarded from the prison to Washington for similar treatment before I saw them. My letters to her were all affectionately preserved.

I am looking at one which I wrote on September 19, 1942. It is an official paper. There is a perforation at the top of the page showing that a portion of the sheet had been torn off. That portion, I suppose, lies in some file in the Department of Justice, duly marked with dates and official memoranda. Reading my letters brings back an acute recollection of my feelings, though the words seem flat and the text disjointed. This one says, in part:

> My dearest Ninele:
> I was happy to receive your first letter; the letter was dated September 2 and came into my hand September 16. . . . I wonder if you get my letters. I hope so. . . . How are you and how are the children? . . . Don't work too much and don't worry too much. I must give you the same advice that you give me. . . . Today I expected you but you did not come. Maybe tomorrow. . . . It is my sincere and earnest hope and wish for you, my dear, that you will have enough to live on and don't have too much trouble and sorrow. What is the church doing? Who will take or is taking my place at this time? . . . My thoughts and prayers are always with you. Sometimes I am convinced you feel it. . . . The Bible is here, my whole consolation. You have your own philosophy, your own world. . . . I read today again the sacerdotal prayer of Christ. (St. John 17) So beautiful and full of divine inspiration. You feel the mystical communion with the eternal Christ when you read His words. . . . Well here is the end again. Sorrow and humor, tears and joy, despair and hope. But above all, Faith and Love! I am longing for you.

The marks I made daily on the door grew into a long file. I examined them critically and was amused at what I could make of them. They looked like soldiers, each with a gun over his shoulder, some with the front foot pressed down, others with the front foot lifted in a kind of goosestep. In fact, by concentrating on them a little, I could give each a separate personality.

My file of soldiers numbered close to thirty when the guard told me to prepare myself for a visit to the warden's office and provided me with a prison outfit that was at least complete and fitted relatively well. I inquired about the meaning of the order and was given no satisfaction until I reached the warden's office. With him was the United States marshal I had met at Hartford. He shook hands with me cordially and asked after my health in a most natural manner. Then he said, "We are going to Lewisburg. I cannot promise you a happy journey, but at least the drive should be pleasant." I went with him out of the room, and down a corridor. The great door of the institution swung back, and we passed into the open air. It was midmorning, the sun was halfway up in a sky of luminous, spotless blue; all around me was light of an unbelievable brilliance, cascading off the roofs of the buildings, being reflected from the ground, and flashing from the leaves on the trees. Space and light seemed boundless. I found myself reaching for the support of walls. There were none. My head spun, I lost my balance, and stumbled. Perhaps I would have fallen if the marshal had not taken me by the arm and supported me till we reached the door of the car waiting at the curb.

The Italian deputy marshal was driving. I sat beside him on the front seat. The marshal and a fourth man sat in the rear. The deputy hailed me in the most friendly fashion and both he and the marshal asked me a few questions about my experience in Danbury as we drove along. I tried to respond in the same spirit but felt unnatural and awkward. A month of solitary confinement does something to your spirit that can't be shed like a coat; moreover, there was the oppressing knowledge that still another jail and additional experiences were awaiting me.

The conversation among the other three men picked up as I withdrew. If it lagged the deputy always took over. He had an unending stream of observations and comments interspersed with an occasional joke, its raciness tempered out of respect for me. Mostly he gossiped of elections and speculated on what the outcome would be in November in this district or that. It was all rather incomprehensible to me and I made no effort to follow it.

There is not much one can say about an automobile ride that has not already been said a hundred times. The route we followed, I learned, was prescribed by the Department of Justice at Washington, but it was of no concern to me what road we took. I was busy becoming accustomed to the feeling of space around me and I kept my attention focused on the endless, smooth, gray-surfaced highway over which we sped with effortless ease. The panorama of hills and woodlands, farms, villages, and towns was always changing, changing so rapidly that it seemed to make no impression whatever upon my memory.

Soon we were in Pennsylvania, which I looked upon as *my* state. What a magnificent state it is! We were in the northeast portion where the hills are high and thickly wooded and the streams hurry along with a copious flow of water. It is a virile countryside but a generous one. The farmhouses and barns looked as content as their well-tended cattle. The villages and towns spoke of plenty and of comfortable living. But in an hour or more we reached the hard-coal country where anthracite like a great black monster had lain at rest in its mausoleum for untold millennia. Now it seemed to be sullenly resentful of the desecration of its grave. It haunted the landscape and touched it with desolation. We entered the busy city of Scranton and stopped for lunch. The sudden halting of the car made the glove compartment flop open. A revolver and a pair of handcuffs were inside, and the revolver fell into my lap. The deputy laughed, picked up the revolver, put it back, and closed the compartment. "Reverend," said the marshal, "you missed a chance for a front-page story."

In the restaurant we had a table for four. I felt conspicuous in my prison garb but my companions ignored it politely and asked me to join them in a drink, which I declined. The most I could master was a cup of coffee. The marshal permitted me to send a post card to my wife; he provided me with both the card and the postage, for I had no money whatever. I insisted that he read what I had written. He merely glanced at it and dropped it in a mailbox.

Some distance beyond Scranton, we passed out of the hard-coal country and were again driving through sweeping hills tinted in many colors. In the embrace of the hills lay great peaceful valleys. The thrill of one could hardly be appreciated before it had vanished with a turn of the road and a new valley and a new arrangement of hills appeared. It was magnificent country lying still and tranquil in the light of a late September day, utterly unconscious of its own magnificence.

Presently the deputy remarked that beyond the hills ahead of us was the Susquehanna River, which we would cross at Sunbury. From there it would be only a few miles to Lewisburg. I remembered that it was also only a few miles from Sunbury to Selinsgrove and Susquehanna University, where I had collected so many pleasing friendships and memories. Life had been full of promise in those days.

The marshal pointed to a tall tower rising above the tree-tops. "There's the 'pen,' and I hope your quarters won't be too bad. At least you'll be surrounded by fine country."

There is a guardhouse at the entrance to the prison grounds.

Beyond it the road winds uphill for perhaps a half-mile. On the left are a number of comfortable homes for the official staff and beyond, at the top of the hill, is the broad front of the prison. The entrance drive makes a wide loop in front of the great doorway, where we stopped. Over the entrance rises a square tower of moderate height, behind which a much higher tower rises into the air to overlook the walled space of the prison and the grounds outside the walls. Looking at the prison, even in my dulled condition I realized that it had been so designed and fitted into the contour of the rolling hilltop as to avoid giving the impression of brutal massiveness. It was nonetheless a jail.

The marshal leaned over and shook my hand. "Goodbye, Reverend. I have no stomach for turning you in. What's the use of having a deputy if you can't get him to do the dirty work?" So the deputy and I got out of the car. We shook hands and said our "goodbyes" before the door opened, for there would not be another chance. The door closed after us and I stood in a high square room under the entrance tower; about ten feet up on the opposite wall was a balcony with a waist-high bulwark—there the guard who controlled the opening of the door was posted. My committment papers were transferred to the prison by the deputy in a thoroughly businesslike manner, then with a curt nod to me he turned and was gone.

7.

'IN THE SHADOW OF
HIS WINGS'

The outside world was shut off, and I was in the custody of the strangers in this new jail where I was committed to spend the next ten years unless something broke the spell. I tried to look through a vista of ten years, a flat vista without markers—nothing but unbroken time. It could not be comprehended.

The strangers quickly took charge of me. I was ordered to pass before an electric eye which would detect any metal on my person, then was turned over along with my commitment papers to a guard who led me out the rear door into an inner court, where a wide strip of well-kept lawn separated the wall from the red brick front of a huge building extending hundreds of feet both to the right and to the left. Here was the jail itself, nestled within the outer walls. The solidity was punctured by many evenly spaced windows.

The guard kept close behind me and directed me to turn and walk along a concrete sidewalk at the base of the wall. I was in no mood for talk and the guard was equally taciturn. I could feel the oppressive presence of the wall, and I noticed the guard towers on top of it and the armed guards within them waiting for action like hunters. The thought occurred to me that the place was a great fortress, its garrison introspectively preoccupied with dominating the enemy in its midst.

The sidewalk turned sharply to the left, crossed the lawn,

and then ran along the side of the three-story building. We went down some steps into the basement and the "receiving room," where my body and my papers were delivered to another guard, a curt fellow who ordered me to strip. He then went over me with a powerful flashlight and examined every hair of my head and every crevice in my skin.

Throughout the proceedings I was conscious of a curious sound that hung in the air about me. It was subdued and I could not identify it at first, but it made me uneasy and sent involuntary shivers down my back. As the examination ended and I started dressing in a newly provided brown prison uniform, there arose against that low background murmur the sound of a Negro's voice chanting a spiritual, heartbreaking in its sorrow. It went on and on, and a choking sob was rising in my throat. Then the voice was drowned, for the background murmur swelled into a great billow of snarls, growls, and curses, accompanied by the beating of metal against metal. The clamor went on as the guard led me up several flights of stairs to the third floor, where he passed me through a steel and glass gate into a passageway. My papers were given to a guard within, who led me through a second steel and glass door into a cell block lined on either side with a row of cells, where fifty or sixty men could be accommodated. He let me into a cell on the east side of the block, closed and locked the heavy door behind me.

My new abode was a rectangle of concrete about five feet wide and nine feet long with an ample steel-barred window set breast-high in the opposite thick wall. Its furnishings consisted of a steel locker, a chair, a toilet, a washbowl, and a cot with freshly laundered covers. The place was harshly rigid, but light and clean. This was my quarantine cell, where I was to be kept for observation to determine both my physical condition and my probable reaction to prison life before being permitted to "enter population."

The sound from below, muffled but distinguishable, followed me in. Slowly it subsided until it was nothing but a remembrance. I learned afterward that it came from what was known as the "hole" on a level lower than the basement receiving room; there men were put for punishment in cells sealed off from all light. The sounds they emit are the cries of primitive man stripped of everything save his bitterness, his hate, and his anguish. I can understand now why the hair on a dog's neck rises and why he growls back at the distant cry of his own kind.

That night I heard the sound again, after nine o'clock, when everyone is ordered to stand before the slit in his door while the guard passes along the corridor making his count. The count had been made and there was a profound stillness in the cell block. I was trying to lose consciousness and was somewhere on the borderline of sleep when that horrid sound pulsed faintly in my ears. At first I thought it was imagination —something drawn out of my memory—but it grew louder and persisted. Soon I heard restless movements in my own cell block, then mutterings. I was fretful myself. I covered my head to shut out the sound but there was a fascination about it and at intervals I uncovered to find out if it was still there. The restlessness and the muttering in our cell block grew; then suddenly from somewhere across the way an agonized voice screamed. The scream formed itself into curses, violent and unspeakably obscene, calling on the damned souls below to stop. Soon the scream was accompanied by pounding on a door and by the beating of heavy objects on a wall. Other voices were added and other poundings. The cell block became an inferno of sound. It was more than just noise. There was a sob in the bitter curses as if they came out of a suffering beyond endurance. How long it carried on I have no idea. I thought it would never cease, but finally it reached a climax and then subsided slowly until it died away in low gasps and sobs. The cell block was still again, and I slept.

The prison siren in the great tower sounded at six A.M. The guard blew a whistle. Ten minutes later he whistled again, and each of us was called upon to stand at the door to be counted. The guard telephoned the results of the count to a central office located in the main corridor, and there was a pause while the tally was checked. When confirmation was received, the locks of our cell doors were released simultaneously by a central switch, and each of us busied himself with broom, mop, and bucket cleaning his own quarters. I noticed that a card had been inserted into a slot on the door of my cell bearing the simple inscription, "Molzahn No. 12150," so that everyone might know the name of the creature confined within. Apparently my reputation had preceded me.

In the cell next to me was a tall Negro with very white teeth. He had a half-sad way of smiling. When our doors were opened, he addressed me as "Reverend" and politely offered to clean my cell. I thanked him but insisted upon doing my own chores. Nevertheless the offer was an opening for conversation and shortly I learned his story. He came from Virginia where he had operated a liquor still somewhere in the woods. Twice the government had shown its disapproval of such enterprise. This, the second time, had brought him to Lewisburg under a two-year sentence. He told me about himself in a modicum of words and a few expressive gestures. His smile seemed to say that it was all a little inscrutable to him. He was not doing anyone harm.

After our work was completed we were lined up for another count, then were marched to breakfast where we served ourselves in a period limited to twenty minutes. We were marched back again; at eight o'clock those prisoners with shop assignments were taken away, and the cell block was empty save for the prisoner who acted as janitor for the block and a few like myself who were unassigned.

I was left to my own thoughts alone in the cell. I stood by the window, reached through the steel bars and opened it. When I did so, autumn seemed to breathe its fragrance in upon me. I looked out over the wooded hills moving away in tumultuous procession to where they merged with the soft blue sky. It seemed that the finest thing in life would be to walk over those hills and lose myself in their spacious grandeur. A feeling of loneliness so acute that it hurt came over me and I had to conjure up thoughts to relieve my feelings.

At Danbury I had read and reread Matthew 26 and 27, which contains the story of the most famous of all trials. It seemed so clear to me now. I could understand the defendant standing aloof and unprotesting, the frightened witnesses giving their halting testimony, the spectators afraid of this man's strange influence, filled with the prejudices which arise out of fear of the incomprehensible, and the judge seeking a judgment that would be discreet in the face of diverse pressures. I thought of that trial entirely apart from its religious significance. Nowhere is the story of legal injustice so succinctly told.

Reading the Bible was one way to control my feelings when I found them getting out of hand; another was to compose a letter to my wife. A degree of poise had to be achieved for the task, for I knew that she was suffering as much or more than I. Three days after my arrival at Lewisburg I wrote to her with an official pencil on an official piece of paper; all the while I had the feeling that the cold eyes of a stranger were looking over my shoulder. My words seemed ineffectual, but I felt that she would understand.

I told her not to worry and quoted to her from the Psalms: "In God have I put my trust, I will not be afraid. . . . In the shadow of his wings will I make my refuge, until these calamities be overpast." I asked her to tell my lawyers where I was, and said I was anxious for news of my appeal. And I tried to communicate my deepest feelings to her:

I can write but two letters to you in thirty days, and in the periods between, my mind is busy with thoughts and words in which to clothe them as tender and loving as any I wrote eighteen years ago, for you are my beloved perhaps even more so now than then, but they refuse to be written, and yet they hover over every word I write however casual it may seem and I know you read them there.

On my first morning at Lewisburg, while my mind was busy with those "thoughts and words," I heard someone call me by name in a low voice. I turned and saw a pair of eyes at the little slit in my cell door. I approached and identified my visitor as the inmate assigned to the job of janitor of the cell block. His cell was next to the entrance, and its door was closed only at night. He stood in the corridor with the long handle of his mop held upright beside him like a spear and began talking eagerly and hurriedly. The guard was responsible for two floors and was apparently not on ours at the time. The janitor began by expressing his sympathy for me in my trouble. He assured me that he had followed the story of my case in the newspapers and had read every word he could find about my trial. And he had read between the lines. He was sure the whole affair was nothing but war hysteria. He told me how the community turned against him during the first world war because of his German descent. "Ah, yes," he concluded, "I know something about war madness."

I thanked him for his sympathy and confidence, which encouraged him to go on. I could see from the vague look in his eyes that he was more involved with something inside of himself than with my problem, and I knew that I was due to hear his story. It took considerable time in the telling and was interrupted more than once, but I shall give it straight through. It was not a novel story. After the war things went reasonably well with him. He became the postmaster of a small town. The salary was not large but with other earnings helped to carry him and his family along, living modestly. Then his daughter was stricken with infantile paralysis. She survived, a cripple. It seemed too much to bear. His interest in life centered upon her and he felt that every remedy must be tried to restore her to soundness. He could not afford to count the cost. Soon his savings were gone, he was hopelessly in debt, and was being pressed for money from many directions. So he took money from the post office and covered up the shortages as long as he could. Ultimately, of course, what he had done was discovered. He fled in terror and lived under an assumed name.

He corresponded with his wife and she urged that he give himself up, which he finally did. He was lodged in a county jail, where conditions must have been bad, for several months. The food officially provided was almost uneatable. The prisoners who had available funds bought their own food. He had no money. The building was old, the cells were clammy and damp. The whole place was ill kept. He became afflicted with a disease which affected his legs. Finally he was taken into court where he pleaded guilty and was given a sentence of three years, less the time already spent in custody. The fact that he had taken the money evidently preyed upon his conscience, and he told me, "I have gone over it again and again in my mind and wonder why I did it, and yet I know, and God knows, that my only child was a cripple."

He looked at me beseechingly as if I carried the power of absolution. Our eyes met. I nodded and said, "Yes, I understand." He seemed about to weep, and then he was gone and I could hear his mop swishing the floor. I went back to my window feeling less lonely but troubled about whether I had said the right thing. I was perplexed as to what the right thing to say might have been.

8.

QUARANTINE

At eleven in the morning we were gathered together and taken to "stockade" for air and sunlight. When I first saw it, stockade was a barren corner of earth, its surface packed hard by countless footsteps. Later it was improved by the inmates with their own hands and their own money (the profits of the commissary) to include a baseball diamond, a grandstand, a grass plot, and facilities for other games.

From it one could see the north or rear wall of the prison enclosure in the middle of which was a guard tower above an entrance closed by a ponderous slab of a gate which could be rolled back only by electric power. Through this gate ran a spur railroad track, on which freight cars entered with the bulk of the prison supplies. Beyond the tracks, near the wall, was the coal pile, an enormous cone of blackness. More removed from the wall was an ample structure housing the prison industries and farther on was the tower which rose to a height that made it a landmark for the country round about. Next came the main prison building which housed me and fifteen hundred others. I had seen the front of it, which faces south, when I entered; now I saw the rear and could begin to organize it in my mind. I was to become as familiar with it as I had been with my own home or church. I arranged the plan of it in my mind by relating the whole structure to the main corridor, which was like a highway running east and west some eight hundred feet. The three-story hospital wing, which included the two quarantine cell blocks and the "Hole," was a transverse bar across its east end, and a similar wing given over to cell blocks I and J crossed its west end. The administration building was on the south side of the prison, at the center, and the dining room was on the north. In the space between the middle and end wings, four three-story wings projected from both the north and south sides of the main structure. They were cell blocks, each designated by a letter.

At the halfway point in the main corridor was the captain's desk rimmed with a high bulwark of shatterproof glass. From that location the entire corridor was under surveillance, and it was impossible to go from one cell block to another without using the corridor. At the desk was a record of all prisoners and a chart showing the preordained movements of each for the day. All inside telephones centered there. It was the nerve center of the prison.

I wandered about stockade rather aimlessly for three-quarters of an hour. I saw the Postmaster. He just greeted me, no more than that, and I wondered whether I had failed him. I was conscious that other prisoners were looking at me with curiosity, but my spirits were low and I had no desire to be sociable.

Another prisoner drew notice to himself by starting to run. He had a long springy stride like a trained runner. The guard who was shepherding us whistled sharply, the guard in the corner tower whistled, a third guard from the center tower joined in the whistling. The fellow kept on running. Our guard cut across his line of travel to intercept him, shouting as he did so, "Hey, you, quit that running." The runner stopped. He was tall, blond, and slender as a lathe.

"Why should I not run?" he queried.

The guard looked at him. "Why shouldn't you run? I am telling you, that's why, it's orders, and I'm giving them to you."

"I do not see any sense in those orders. I am not running away, I am just getting exercise."

"Getting exercise! Good God! See those guards up there? They got guns and they're trigger happy. Any more of your damned exercise and you'll be drilled full of holes, and I don't want that happening on my shift. Another thing—see that white line, ten feet inside the wall? Don't cross it! Stay away from that wall or you'll fetch up on a slab in the morgue."

The tall fellow shrugged his shoulders as if to say, "Have it your way, but it doesn't make sense."

I was still confined to my cell the following morning after the cell block had been largely emptied by those departing for job assignments. Again I heard the swish of the mop coming along the corridor and the scraping of the bucket as it was moved along the concrete floor. The sound stopped beside my door and I once more faced the Postmaster through the narrow slit. Once again we were engaged in conversation. The Postmaster had been thinking things over and was disturbed by his confidences of the day before, so our conversation took an entirely different slant. This time he wanted to impress upon me that he had no use for ministers or churches. Priests and pastors were hypocrites and spineless yes-men who catered to the rich and bowed before worldly authority. They were complacent when they should be courageous. They preached the words of Christ but had forgotten their meaning. Their teachings were derived from the Bible, but they themselves had lost the spirit of the Holy Book. Only for the Quakers did he have a good word. They had simplicity and courage, and he quoted, "Theirs is a faith that overcomes the world." As for most of the other churches, he judged, "Theirs is a faith that is overcome by the world." The church of Rome he considered a great organization distinctly of this world, and he assured me that as one of its priests I would never have been left to suffer such adversity.

In the course of our conversation it became clear that he was a close student of the Bible with a retentive memory. I never attempted to contradict him, but tried to show him something of the problem from the viewpoint of the minister. Of necessity the church has a worldly aspect, and the proper adjustment of this to the spiritual is a problem that has never been solved satisfactorily. I asked that he not prejudge me and said that I should be given a fair trial. If he found me wanting, he should tell me frankly what I lacked.

We had several more days in which to converse in the empty cell block. On his next appearance he brought four treasured letters from his wife. It seemed that, having made it clear to me what he thought of ministers, he could again give me his confidence. He read portions of the letters. His wife was going along, but the going was not easy. I could understand what was in his mind. He was thinking that it was not the prisoner who suffered the most, it was those who were left in the outside world and had to carry on in the battle of life.

Another morning he silently passed me by several times before he spoke. His eyes looked even sadder than usual. I could see that he was gripping the mop handle tightly. In his ill-fitting prison suit of brown khaki, he looked cast more for comedy than for a tragic role, and yet he emanated tragedy. Then he told me that today was his fiftieth birthday, as well as his twenty-fifth wedding anniversary. He and his wife had planned a celebration a year ago and had invited relatives and friends to attend. Now all he had for the occasion was a letter from his wife. He gave it to me to read. It was filled with affection and words of cheer. One passage I remember. It said, "Darling, since you have been taken away from me the world is not the same, the sun is not the same, the flowers have lost their charm, and our bed is cold and lonely." When I passed the letter back to him through the slit, I noticed tears on his cheeks. He shook his head sharply, picked up his bucket, shouldered his mop, and in a moment was out of my sight. He might not have been garbed for tragedy, but I could see nothing comic in his figure.

Strangely enough, now that I was sharing someone else's sorrow, the edge was being taken off my own. The Postmaster had broken through the cloak of reserve which I had wrapped about me, and I found that now I was instinctively taking an interest in my fellows. Almost directly across the corridor was the cell of the tall runner of the stockade, who was in frequent dispute with our guard, whose speech and appearance marked him unmistakably as an Irishman. In the morning, when we were called upon to stand at the slit in the door to be counted, the guard would stop at the runner's cell and I could hear his gruff voice. "Hey, you! Get up here to the door."

The runner apparently did not approve of a 6 A.M. reveille and from within would come an answer couched in English with an unmistakable German base overlayed with an Oxford accent. I too had learned my English with that accent. The voice would be patiently explanatory, the words precisely formed:

"I am here, am I not? And you see me and you can count me—that should be sufficient."

It clearly was not, for an indignant official explosion followed, to the effect that orders were orders, and rules were rules.

Then again the clipped accent: "Now, my dear fellow, you must see for yourself that the rule is a foolish one."

There would be another official outburst and another answer and the climax would come when the guard discovered he had forgotten the count. This called for bitterness:

76

"You damn lazy loafer. You've made me do my count over again. So help me, if you're not up here when I come back, you'll do a stretch in the Hole."

The cell block enjoyed the dispute, particularly the last part. The voice within the cell could not be heard throughout the whole block, but everyone with his ear cocked to the slit could hear the guard's part of it.

After several days of trouble the guard brought his superior officer along with him, and they were closeted for a while with the runner—then that particular difficulty ceased. I was told that the debate was vigorous, but was terminated by their success in pointing out to the runner that the guard did not make the rules and their assurance that a complaint to the warden would afford an opportunity to present the case to the proper authorities. This was an example of the prison's much referred-to co-operation between inmate and the custodial staff. Some guards had a way of maintaining discipline with a minimum of disciplinary action, considered to be in their favor by the prison authorities.

As we marched to the dining room in pairs I sometimes saw the runner. He carried his head high and with rather an arrogant bearing. Once when we were paired together he spoke to me. He knew my name, and I had been curious enough to learn his by looking at the card on his door. He referred to himself as "Baron," but he was quite gracious to me and mentioned some of my father's relatives whom he had known in Germany. I learned that upon coming to this country he had engaged in the business of importing precious stones, apparently with considerable success. He had married an American girl and lived in a fashionable area. He was a devotee of sports and played polo. After the war broke out, although he was a naturalized citizen, the government seized his money and prosecuted him under the Trading with the Enemy Act, and here he was. He seemed quite undaunted and was confident the error would be corrected by his appeal to a higher court. As we walked together, he launched into a criticism of a number of the prison regulations which he thought unnecessary and obnoxious, and assured me that he intended to protest to the warden at the first opportunity.

The contrast of personalities in the jail was striking. In the cell next to the Baron was another prisoner who also managed to impress himself upon his fellows. He was a loud-mouth; his thoughts seemed to be concocted in a sewer and he expressed them at every opportunity. I could hear him at times standing at the slit in his cell door shouting jokes and comments to his unseen audience. At other times he would busy himself by drawing foul pictures and scribbling obscene verses on the toilet paper in his cell, which he circulated when we were let out of our cell. He was a startling phenomenon. The Postmaster, who, as janitor, picked up all kinds of news, told me that this "phenomenon" had been engaged in some form of white-slave traffic.

Further down the block was a sturdy little blond fellow as inarticulate as the others were vocal. The janitor told me that he was a German sailor rumored to have been connected with the Long Island saboteurs. Having followed that story in the press, I wondered how he could have possibly fitted into it. I never had a chance to find out, for he talked to no one and shortly after my arrival left quarantine. Months later I was to see him again under circumstances carrying the ultimate in tragedy for him.

There were many others, of course, but since they did not participate in my subsequent life in the jail other than as familiar faces glimpsed in "population," I shall let them pass.

It had been Wednesday when I arrived at Lewisburg. It was Sunday before special attention was given me; I was taken to the hospital for registration, and my entire history was reviewed and recorded. On Monday began a series of examinations. First I stood stripped with several other prisoners waiting for a surgeon who was a half-hour late. When he arrived he shot his questions at us as if he resented us one and all. What an ill-tempered fellow he appeared to be! I thought he seemed particularly malicious toward me, as though by striking at my defenseless nakedness he was striking at an enemy he hated. It was amost too much to bear, but I succeeded in making myself impassive by considering the episode as a mere trifle in the infinity of time.

Next there was an educational director who was supposed to determine the nature of the work to which I should be assigned. He was as rude as the surgeon was vicious. He bore me a special grudge, and told me in passing, "Fellows like you would be shot in Germany. You're lucky that we are sentimental fools." I felt that he envisioned my execution with satisfaction. He recorded my answers to his ordinary questions in a spiteful way, making it clear that he thought the whole business was a waste of time.

Then I was turned over to the director of gymnastics, a former football player who treated me decently. The only question of his that I remember was that of what sports I had participated in. I could hit upon only one, so I told him that my sport was horseback riding, the incongruity of which under the circumstances appeared to both of us as humorous.

The librarian, who was next in line, inquired about my taste in books. He, too, resented me for a Nazi and was bitterly sarcastic throughout the interview, apparently hating every minute of it. Was I a slow or rapid reader? Was I systematic or desultory? I told him that at the time I was having difficulty concentrating on anything I read and that about all I could master were parts of the New Testament.

I passed on to the aptitude test and felt how absurdly inadequate my equipment was for the ordinary affairs of life. When I came to that part of the test which consisted of looking at a inkblot on a piece of paper and describing what I saw in it, I felt too foolish to go on.

The tail end of the gauntlet consisted of two interviews, one with the psychologist and one with the psychiatrist. Both men were Jews. The first was considerate and courteous. We later became friends, and he even had occasion to seek me out for advice on intimate domestic matters which troubled him, but the other drew away from me as if I were unclean.

At last it was all over. Whether it took one or more days I do not recall, but it seemed to me I had been pushed through a shredder so many times that there was not the tiniest fold of privacy left to me. Several days later I appeared before the prison board, which met in a room in the administration wing. I was given a pass by the quarantine guard which let me out the gate down the stairs and into the main corridor. My pass was checked and rechecked all along the way. Then I sat on a bench in the passageway until my turn came to enter the meeting room.

The prison board sat at a table which was small enough to afford informality. Around it were the warden, the associate and assistant wardens, three parole officers, the Roman Catholic and Protestant chaplains, the chief doctor of the hospital, and a stenographer. I sat with them and was submitted to questioning. I appreciated the fact that this interviewing was primarily for the purpose of enabling the staff to become acquainted with each of its charges, and I answered as briefly and as courteously as I was able. Then one of my interviewers asked, "What was the nature of your crime?" He was the only one of the group I knew. I had been introduced to him at Hartford while my trial was in progress and before I became a convict. He knew my case well. His inquiry nettled me somewhat, and I replied promptly, "I committed no crime and you know it," for I had resolved never to permit a suggestion that I had committed a crime pass unchallenged.

The interview proceeded without further reference to the matter. At its conclusion I was asked whether I had any preference as to a work assignment or to living quarters (dormitory or separate cell) when I entered population. This was another matter about which I had made a previous resolution. I replied, "Gentlemen, I am in your custody. The reason for my being here is a matter with which you have no direct concern. You have a duty to perform. I shall comply with your directions to the best of my ability, but those directions are to be given by you. I do not wish to express preferences."

The interview was over. It may be that my resolution reflected stubbornness, but I felt that I was entitled to an expression of my own ideas, for I was resolved to take anything that might come without complaining.

9.

LIFE IN H-3

The next day, as nearly as I can remember, I was called upon to report for work with the others at the sound of the eight o'clock siren. I was part of a group marched to the industries building in front of which sat several railroad cars on the spur track, loaded with sheets of stainless steel destined for the prison shops where they would be fashioned into many shapes. My conception of the size and complexity of the prison's industrial plant was expanding. I also learned of the precautions taken to make sure that none of the inmates departed through the stone slab along with the train. Both the cars and the locomotive were first inspected with the greatest care; then they waited outside of the wall within a second enclosure until the population of the jail had been counted and the whereabouts of everyone reported. Even in the face of those precautions escapes had occurred, I was told.

Once, just as the locomotive was pulling out, it was captured by three or four desperate men who sent it charging through the gate, depending on the massive weight of their captured machine to crush opposition. Outside the gate the track passed over a pit, and the track could be dropped down by pulling an electric switch in the guard tower. The preposterous had been anticipated and prepared for. An alert guard pulled the switch and the locomotive piled up in the pit. The escape was foiled. Any way you look at it, the odds against its success had been overwhelming, but it had offered

the thrill of the gamble over against the fretting dulness of
prison life.

The work gang to which I was assigned was ordered to un-
load the freight cars. The logic of my assignment here was
disturbing. I could only conclude that all of my interviews and
aptitude tests had added up to zero, so I was given the first
job that came to hand. If I had been twenty or twenty-five
years younger I might have become adept at this manual labor
after a brief apprenticeship and in time perhaps achieved an
amazing muscular development (like Jean Valjean in *Les
Miserables*). But it was a bit too late in life for me to start.
I tried, but I felt utterly incompetent and awkward.

The Baron was on the same shift. He was younger than I
and sinewy, but not built for heavy lifting; nevertheless, he
tried to look after me, which I appreciated. We wore overalls,
stiff with grease, and gloves, already badly torn, to protect our
hands, for the sharp edges of the steel could cut cruelly. I did
not last long—three or four days at the most—when a strip
of steel fell on my foot and I was taken to the hospital hu-
miliated at my own ineptitude and suffering considerable discomfort.

Fortunately the injury was not serious, and soon I was
ready for my next assignment—peeling potatoes and onions
in the kitchen. That too, I thought sardonically, seemed appropriate to the sum of my accomplishments. I had a companion of apparently similar aptitude for this work—a little
old man with a handkerchief tied about his head. He wore a
brown quarantine suit and I remembered having seen him on
our way to meals. He paid no attention to me. His head was
bent over his task. I could hear him talking to himself. His
conversation obviously was not a happy one, for tears were
running down his wrinkled cheeks, and not from the onions.
His voice was low-pitched, but soon I ascertained that he was

reciting lamentations in Hebrew. After a while I spoke to him in that language. He gave me a quick frightened look, and stopped his muttering. I felt I had intruded on his privacy. After a while I spoke again, this time in German, and apologized for interrupting him. He brightened at the familiar sounds and answered me. Before long we were engaged in conversation and I discovered that he knew who I was, so I was spared an explanation of what brought me to prison.

This discussion touched on our respective families, and presently he was fully launched upon a description of his own, which then led to the story of his misfortune, which had arisen in connection with some financial matters. I was none too clear at the time exactly what these were and even less clear now, but I got the impression that he himself was confused about them. He was a rabbi and had been in this country but a short time. His story was accompanied by the shrugging of his shoulders and the quick movement of his hands. He told me of the unutterable sorrow he felt at being separated from his family, the thought of which had given rise to his tears. All of them had just been getting a start in the promising new world when this thing happened to him. He broke anew into lamentations and tears. I managed to shift the conversation to the old Hebrew prophets; here he was on familiar ground and soon was talking about them in a most engaging way. The week or more that I was assigned to the kitchen I remember as seasoned with the sting of onions and the lore of ancient Israel.

Prisoners live by strict schedule. The official day started at six every morning with the siren that permeated every corner of the jail. We were counted at 6:15. We were marched to and from breakfast exactly as the schedule demanded. We were called to work by the siren exactly at eight, and we worked fixed hours to the tick of the clock. We sauntered in the stockade, we rested, all according to the clock. We were counted and recounted like sheep. Each of us at every moment of the day fitted into a preordained spot where he could be located at once. We seemed to live with guards at our elbows. We went to the library at a fixed time. We were told from on high when we should go to the barber.

I shall not forget the first time it was ordained that I should have my hair cut. I was given a pass and carried it down the stairs to the corridor. The captain's desk had been notified of the time of my departure and my destination. I walked half the length of the corridor to the near end of the captain's desk, where my arrival was checked. I went down to the basement where I found the barbershop where the operation was performed. The adventure was impressed upon my memory, for on my return I found new orders awaiting me. I was directed to Clothing Issue, which was located in the basement beside the barbershop. There I received a blue suit in exchange for my brown khaki.

We were not to be seen by the outside world in prison brown, and I was to have a visitor. My wife was calling upon me that day. Deeply affected by this news, I once again emerged with a pass which took me along the central corridor past the captain's desk and into an anteroom where I was "frisked" to make sure I carried no papers or messages or anything lethal. I knew I would have to become used to such treatment, but I could never quite get over the feeling of abasement those searches gave me.

At last I was admitted to the spacious visiting room, fitted with a large flat table in the shape of a horseshoe. On one side sat the prisoner in penal territory, on the other the visitor in free territory. A partition about fifteen inches high ran down the center of the table like a dorsal fin. Anything exchanged between visitor and prisoner had to pass over its top in view of the guard, who sat at the end of the horseshoe. I was directed to take my position close to the end of the table to be under the surveillance of that guard. Perhaps I should have been proud that I had been rated so highly. Washington considered me a particularly dangerous man. I could see my wife seated on her side of the table with the guard almost at her elbow. I took a seat on my side of the table facing her.

Our conversation was hurried and full of meaning to us. There was so much I wanted to hear: How was she making out? How were the children doing? What was going on at the church and who was conducting the services in my absence? The half-hour allotted to us seemed unbelievably short. Then I was on my way back to my cell and she on her tedious journey to Philadelphia. Her faithfulness in coming to visit me I shall never forget.

I returned to Clothing Issue to change back into my quarantine suit and there found further orders. I was to retain my blue suit and be transferred to population. Moreover, I was to have a new job, that of a clerk-trainee in Clothing Issue itself. I was directed to go to cell block H-2 at seven P.M. with all my belongings. My permanent dormitory was to be the floor above, H-3, but there was no space for me at that time and there was a vacant cot on the second floor. Shortly before seven I wrapped up a toothbrush, a razor, and a comb in my bedding, took my identification card out of its slot, and made my way with my pass to the guard at cell block H-2 who opened a final gate and let me inside the dormitory.

It was a long room with a double row of cots, heads to the wall. In a wide aisle between the rows there were tables where men sat playing cards. Beyond the tables, the aisle was occupied by a second row of cots, head to head. There were some forty-five to fifty men in the room, scattered about in many postures, some on their cots engaged in conversation, some playing checkers on the tops of the steel lockers which lay between each pair of cots. A number turned to stare at me as I came in, and I speculated on my reception.

My cot was but a short distance from the door. The guard watched while I slipped my card into the slot prepared for it at the cot's foot. Then he left me. The mattress of my cot was turned up toward the wall. I went to turn it down. A man lounging on the cot just beyond mine watched. Apparently he reached a decision and got up saying, "Here! I'll give you a hand." He grasped one side of the mattress, and together we unrolled it and set it in place. Then he helped me with the remainder of the simple operation of getting settled, talking freely as he did so. He kept on talking after the operation was completed. He informed me that they all knew about my case in the dormitory and had followed the story of the trial carefully. There was a difference of opinion, "but mostly," he said, "we thought the works were in against you." Then he managed to slip over into his own story:

"I ought to know something about that. The administration gave me the same sort of deal. My business was in Washington, and I had a mighty good thing. I knew a lot of the right people—thought I was in on the ground floor—but some guy got down under me in the cellar and here I am. I think you'll be all right in this dormitory. We have sort of a top man. A great guy. He used to know every angle in the outside world and he knows every angle in this place. I'll introduce you to him. If he treats you all right, you're O.K."

He nodded to me to come with him, and we walked to the first table in the aisle, where four men were playing cards. My escort addressed one of the players by a nickname, obviously proud of the privilege of such an intimacy. He said, "That Lutheran minister is here. You ought to meet him." A man with his back to us put down his cards carefully and arose.

We were introduced and shook hands. His was a widely known name even before it was headlined when he became a defendant in a criminal prosecution—an income tax case, as I recall it. I looked him over with interest. He was several inches taller than I and carried himself with a grace and style that showed even in his prison garb—a man who knew all the angles might have a specially fitted suit. He was, I judge, about sixty years of age. About him was a natural air of distinction and command. He looked at me searchingly and, I suppose, measured me as I measured him. But I am sure I presented no such imposing figure. I was also conscious of the fact that everyone in the room was looking at us. When he spoke his voice had a deep musical tone:

"We have been reading about you, Reverend, and some of us here think the government gave you a rough passage, but don't let it get you down—and above all don't think too much."

I thanked him and said, "It isn't easy not to think, but I believe I have myself pretty well in hand."

He continued the conversation: "I understand we both drew ten-year sentences, but my lawyers are working to get me out. I suppose yours are doing the same." He smiled. "Mine tell me that they will keep right on fighting for my release if it takes them ten years. Better luck than that to you."

The interview was over. He went back to his cards and I to my cot. The room relaxed. Everyone seemed satisfied to go back to what he was doing. The Top Man had approved of me.

My next-door neighbor who had sponsored the affair seemed quite happy about it and became very communicative. He told me a long story of Washington intrigues and how well he had been doing because he knew his way around. He spoke familiarly of all the prominent names in the government—apparently all intimates of his. The story was entirely too intricate for me to follow so I assented without dispute to its ultimate conclusion, that the Department of Justice had played a dirty trick upon him when it shipped him off to Lewisburg.

The dormitory lights went out at nine o'clock, but the room was only half-dark because of dim lights kept on inside and the floodlights outside, which illuminated the entire prison grounds except when there was a blackout during air-raid alerts. That light streamed through our windows. Nevertheless, I slept.

When the eight o'clock siren sounded to send us off to work I reported for duty to the officer in charge of Clothing Issue. I found him to be a red-headed fellow, with an extraordinary voice—his whisper approximated an average man's speaking voice and his ordinary voice was an average man's shout. When I presented myself and my papers he looked over both and then shouted, to no one in particular, "So they sent me a goddamned Nazi spy, and I got seven kikes who would like to slice him into bacon. What do they expect me to do about it?" He took a step or two and then shouted at me, "Well, get into the cage there and go to work. May God help you if those sons-of-bitches go to work on you." It was not a cheering introduction to my new assignment, but I was buried all of that first day in a smother of clothes and shoes and miscellaneous items of equipment in my wire cage. I had little chance to see anything else and my associates could not see me.

During the day I wondered occasionally how I was going to be received in H-3, my permanent dormitory, that evening, but my experience of the night before was reassuring. At seven o'clock I took my little bundle of belongings from H-2 and started up the stairs. The guard opened the gate into the room and accompanied me to a vacant cot. Then he departed. The place had the same appearance and equipment as the one below. Its occupants were lolling about in many attitudes. I was conscious that I was the center of attention and had a creepy feeling that the eyes focused upon me were hostile. The mattress was turned up against the wall in the usual way. When I took hold of it and turned it down a great clatter arose. Inside was a miscellaneous collection of old shoes, papers, empty tobacco tins, and stones apparently brought in from stockade.

Someone behind me laughed harshly. Another mocked, "Did you hear what the Reverend said?" and someone else, "Caught in a booby trap—he's a hell of a spy."

I was feeling very uncomfortable but said nothing. I took what I could of the mess in both hands and walked down the passage between the cots to a rubbish can near the entrance and deposited my load. I was most deliberate. Time was a commodity of which I had an unlimited supply and I used it liberally. The eyes followed me. I noticed in particular one redheaded man sitting on the edge of his cot, eyeing me intently. I never saw a face more expressive of concentrated emotion—it was incandescent with hate. I made three trips to the rubbish can. When I returned from the last trip the young fellow who had the cot next to mine—the name on his card was Italian—spoke to me. He had a disdainful tone in his voice, which he was at no pains to lower:

"Don't pay any attention to that redheaded kike. He's been working all day to line this place up against you, but he hasn't got us all even so."

Another man joined us, a Jew. "That's right," he said, "Don't pay attention to that kike. He's nothing but a crook."

He moved on when a third man came up. These last two, I later learned, were brothers, but they did not speak to each other. This one talked to me reassuringly, and as he did so I was listening to something that clung to his words. Then I had it.

"East Prussia?" I said.

"Ya! Ya!" he replied brightly.

"Pomerania," I remarked.

"Ah!" and his voice ran up and down the scale. Then he broke into German and soon I had his story. Thirty years ago they had come from the old country, Mama and Papa and the brothers. The parents were both dead. The brothers had been brothers both in blood and in action. They had lived together, worked together, made money together . . . then a bitter look came over his face: "Ach, what a brother!"

As I made my bed I could hear someone walking toward us with an uneven step. It was the Postmaster, the janitor from quarantine, and he helped me complete my task. The gesture lined him up on my side. He had preceded me into the dormitory by a day or so.

The young Italian sat in the middle of his cot with his back supported by a pillow. He watched us working for a while without comment. Then he made a gesture with his hand toward my neighbor on the other side whose back was set toward me and spoke:

"Look at the Rabbit. What a man! He says he made thirty million dollars on the outside and some of it's still waiting for him. But that kike gets him hopped up and there he sits hating you. Don't let it bother you. He has pictures of his yacht in his locker and pictures of himself all decked out in white yachting clothes, and pictures of himself with his distinguished guests. He won't stick to the hate program. You'll see those pictures soon enough, and that'll be your hard luck."

I glanced at the man's back. It seemed that the speaker was right. The back was definitely hostile, and it stood up rigidly against the words of contempt leveled against it.

A well-built young man joined us. He had a haggard face marked with lines that usually come with age. Not far behind him was a tall slender fellow, also young; his face was sensitive and drawn to the edge of hysteria. Both told me of their grave concern at my being there and assured me that they had followed my case carefully in the newspapers and were convinced that I was a victim of a great injustice. It occurred to me that there was a distinct advantage in being such a notorious criminal—it spared me much explaining. Four people had joined me now at the cot, in addition to my friendly neighbor, who could if he chose be part of the group or withdraw from it without changing his position.

As always the conversation gravitated to the matters that were uppermost in the mind of each. Soon I learned that the chubby little fellow out of East Prussia nursed the conviction that he was the miserable victim of his brother's wrongdoing. They had been lithographers; they were charged with infringing on the government's prerogatives by lithographing internal revenue stamps, and they were convicted.

The young Italian thought of himself as a prize exhibit illustrating a stupid system of justice. His case had involved certain deals in stocks which had been explained most fully to show their legitimacy as business transactions before a jury which knew nothing of stocks or business transactions. The prosecuting attorney talked the jury's language and was interested in nothing but his record of convictions.

The two young fellows were conscientious objectors. They were unconcerned with the processes responsible for their confinement and were interested only in the rectitude of their own beliefs in a world that had deserted Christ, the Savior, and had gone mad in the pursuit of false gods. They accepted what they considered their martyrdom without protest. Their faith lived so strongly in them that it seemed about to consume them. They were eager to talk about it with me, not in order to make a convert, certainly not to have me show the way to bring their doctrines into harmony with the world, but only because the subject was the center of their thoughts and talking about it enabled them to think of new ways of expressing their own belief to themselves. They knew the Bible and were ready with text and citation to support their position. I was left to argue the cause of the world and my own cause as well, for my record as a soldier was involved.

The young man with the haggard face, known as the Kid, had come out of his father's home to the penitentiary. He was nineteen. The other, known as the Swede, was a native of the Middle West but had been arrested and sentenced somewhere near New York City. He was twenty-three. Both had refused to register under the draft law. The Kid, in expressing his convictions, had hurt his father gravely; all his relatives had abandoned him, some accusing him of cowardice. The Swede had been living not with his family but in a communal unit patterned on the teachings of primitive Christianity. He had been an actor filling small parts.

If I protested that one's duty to others sometimes called for great sacrifices, the inevitable reply came that the Savior said, "Forsake all and follow me." The discussion went on, as all such discussions must, in an inconclusive grappling between the real and the unreal.

All this talk wearied the chubby little man from East Prussia, who drifted away, and the young Italian, who withdrew into himself and observed us with aloof disdain. When finally my visitors were gone he had this comment: "Those two friends of your were probably all right once, but they ate something too strong for them, and now they're nuts."

For all practical purposes he was undoubtedly right, but I could not dispose of the two so readily. In a way they symbolized both the greatness of mankind and its capacity for sublime tragedy. Those among us who see visions and follow them are those who lead mankind out of the slough. Some achieve greatness, haunted by tragedy, and project their shadows over centuries of history, but most achieve merely tragedy, petty and futile in the eyes of all except those who suffer it. Fortunately, few see visions beyond the sight of the rest of us.

It was nine o'clock. The scream of the siren filled the room, the bright lights went off while the dim ones remained on and, aided by the light from outside, enabled us to see the length of the room, shrouded in shadows. The games were stopped, the cards returned to the guard who issued them. Every man was in his cot or standing at its foot to answer the tally of the guard as he walked the length of the room making his evening count.

I wanted to forget myself in sleep. In H-2 the Top Man had made it known that he did not like to be disturbed after retiring. The quiet there was comforting, but in H-3 there was no such top man, and from the cots arose a miasma of conversation. There was one outstanding voice which came from somewhere across the room giving utterance to vile thoughts and arousing raucous laughter. I knew the voice. I had heard it in quarantine. It was that of the White Slaver. Other voices arose insisting on a hearing, all equally vile. Among them was that of my enemy down the line, who drew his material from the Moslem East and the sewers of the old cities of Europe. In his stories he was always the great spender sought after by everyone. I heard the young Italian mutter, "The lying bastard. He has been in Turkey, though. He's wanted by the police there."

The talk went on and on; it was nearly two o'clock when it died away, but even in sleep that wretched dormitory was not quiet. Many of the men were past middle age and some snored prodigiously, none more so than my neighbor the Rabbit. Now and again a distressed sleeper would start up cursing, and a missile would come sailing through the air in the direction of the noise. Sometimes it fetched the Rabbit, sometimes me. There were many who muttered in their sleep or cried out loud. The Swede at times would start up with a shriek which was filled with such stark terror that it would grip you at the throat. All through the night there were stealthy flittings of the degenerate ones engaged in their revolting practices.

Fifty or more of us were in that dormitory, each harboring an unhappy spirit. We were a human pool, stagnant and loathsome.

10.

CLOTHING ISSUE

I gathered myself together in the morning and took my place in line to make use of the washing and shaving facilities in the washroom at the end of the dormitory.

At the eight o'clock siren, I went downstairs to the corridor. Men in drab blue uniforms were emerging from every cell block. The guards marshaled us into a long thin column, two abreast, where talking was forbidden. We marched along the corridor, and the column diminished as we went to our respective destinations. I left at the stairs to the basement on the north side of the corridor. Near the foot of those stairs was the entrance to Clothing Issue. I entered with others and was greeted by my vociferous officer:

"You can go to the clerk's desk today. He won't be in." Then, apparently for his audience, "This place don't smell like a church chancel at a wedding, but if you've got a strong stomach you may get to like it."

It was his idea of humor and was accepted with laughter by the other inmates who were entering with me. But as he pointed out, the atmosphere in the room was not appealing to one's stomach. The ventilation was none too good. It became worse as the weather grew colder, for the heat came from steam pipes just under the ceiling; when they were working the upper air was oppressively warm while the lower was chilly and damp. This arrangement was the subject of many critical outbursts from our officer, who cursed his superiors without restraint as well as the army doctors who had rejected him for service.

"I had a commission in the first war," he told us, "and I'd have been sitting pretty in this one if it hadn't been for those doctors. So here I am in this hole where I sweat from my neck up and freeze from my knees down. The Krauts couldn't do any worse by me. I'll be crawling around on my hands and knees pretty soon with carbuncles for joints."

The air was laden with heavy odors of sweaty clothes, sweaty leather, and other, unidentifiable objects. As you entered there was a wire cage on the right guarding racks of clothes which I learned were civilian outfits for inmates about to go out again into the outside world. On the left was a space enclosed by a waist-high rail; at the far end were two flat-topped desks, the one by the outer rail for the officer in charge, that on the inside for his clerk. The railed-off space was backed by a wire cage, which was my immediate charge. Its contents consisted of officers' shoes on the shelves and officers' clothing on the racks, which crowded the cage to suffocation.

Seated at either of the two desks one had a view of the whole domain. Directly across the passageway within a cage was the desk of the custodian for civilian clothing. At it sat the prisoner who had that duty—he was none other than my redheaded enemy from H-3. Beyond the cages, in a central space, was a long table where sat the prisoners who distributed bedding and the other miscellaneous articles for prison use. Behind them were three compartments, one stuffed chock full of the material they handed out; the middle one was given over to the shoemakers and the third to the tailors.

I was kept reasonably busy waiting on officers. They would walk directly into my cage and start helping themselves to shoes. If they wanted new clothes, I measured them and found a suit that would fit. Some seemed to take pleasure in humiliating me. One in particular, the officer in charge of the barbershop next door, carried on a one-sided conversation meant for me which he made as blasphemous and sacrilegious as his vocabulary permitted. He and some of the others took both shoes and clothing without signing a receipt. At first I permitted this on the theory that it was not the function of a prisoner to give instructions to an officer—a prisoner was a low form of life without rights. When my boss heard of it he shouted me down:

"Those guys are thieves, by god, and that son-of-a-bitch from the barbershop would sell his mother if the price was right. Shoes are at a premium outside. Make the bastards sign—every last one of them." So I did from that time on.

It was made clear to me that I was nothing more than a clerk trainee, understudy of the clerk himself. My own desk was inside the cage with the officers' equipment, while the clerk's desk was outside. This I was to occupy only when the clerk was not about, which was most of the time; the man who had this position was anticipating an early release and was engaged in learning the Morse code with the idea that the army would call for his services. When I first met him I was struck by the fact that the dome of his head seemed as broad as his shoulders. I could understand why he was called Jughead. He had bright eyes that glittered when he was elaborating an idea, and he was always having ideas. They would grow like a magician's flowers as he talked. One of them was to write a treatise on jails called "Men in Jail"—it would be a masterpiece. It would tear the walls down so that all the world could look inside and see what a jail was like. Jughead had been a newspaper man and a free-lance writer, and he graciously included me as a collaborator in the project.

The redheaded officer was within hearing range when this

proposal was made; after Jughead departed, he grunted, "He ought to be able to write about jails—he's been in and out of 'em for the last ten years. That fellow's got brains. Has an idea a minute and he can sell them too, and that's the root of the trouble. Every one of his ideas has a catch in it. Somebody gets stuck, and it isn't Jughead. You can't get blood out of a turnip. But he gets the bite when the cops catch up with him."

The officer wasn't through with his analysis. "You heard him just now. You can see what I mean. If he sold you his idea, pretty soon you'd be staking him to a trip to get firsthand information on federal jails from Alcatraz on east. But when he got the money, he'd get a new idea and you'd never see him again until the money ran out and he came drifting back to his old haunts. Would he have meant to cheat you? You wouldn't know, and like as not he wouldn't either. Maybe he believes in his own ideas. I don't know, but I do think he's too screwy for a jail. You can't keep him out, though, and he's not screwy enough for a nuthouse. What can you do with a bastard like that?

"Now he's full of the idea that the army wants him. I say, give him to the army along with our Paddy, the shoemaker. Paddy has as many fingers as a centipede and they're so nimble you can't see them work. The army ought to drop that pair back of the enemy lines; with Jughead's brains and Paddy's fingers they could steal anything. Hitler would be likely to wake up some morning and find the Berchtesgarten missing."

When I was at the outside desk I could look into the inner recesses of Clothing Issue and see the tailors bending over their tasks, the shoemakers crouched on their stools like toads, the custodians of the general stock in their crowded compartment, and the distributors sitting behind the long table. Our customers were largely inmates who came in with passes and requisitions. Our officer received them tilted back in his swivel chair with his feet on the rail. He would take the pass, twist his long wrist to note the time on his watch, mark it on the pass, issue an order to someone over his shoulder, and give the inmate directions.

Conversation among the workers in Clothing Issue flowed endlessly, and it rarely got out of the gutter. I was a new subject for discussion that was seized upon quickly. I could hear the sneering voice of my redheaded enemy across the way:

"Muffle your mouths, you sinners, we got a holy one among us." And an answer, "Well I'll be damned," and still another, "A Nazi minister with a special message from Hitler to *Unser Gott.*"

The voices went on, each adding its contribution; then someone said, "Get him to pray for us," and another, "Hey Nazi, you got a connection with God, use it to get us out of this hell-hole."

When I didn't answer, a bitter voice screamed, "Down on your knees, you bastard—down on your knees, pray as you've never prayed before, pray us out of this Godforsaken place."

A pause, then another voice, harsh and sardonic, "If you won't pray, go into your act. Deliver a sermon for us lost souls. Put it on thick—maybe we'll hit the trail."

"Plant some dolls along it," came another, "and I'll hit any trail." Still another voice amended, "Dolls . . . by god, I'll settle for less. Anything that looks like a woman'll do."

Here was a diversion, bringing up a subject that constantly obsessed them. But they came back to me intermittently, day after day. There were tedious repetitions and sometimes embellishments. An inmate coming for a blanket or something else would be given the news about the Reverend, and the record would be played over again, or someone would think up a new insult to me and my calling, and the chain reaction would be set off again among the others. Eventually, after some weeks, the game lost its flavor. I never gave them the satisfaction of knowing that I listened to them.

When on occasion our officer was away from our room on some business, the conversation usually took on a different twist. Heated arguments arose over the "take," which I discovered consisted of cartons of cigarettes, the prison's "currency." I began to comprehend some of the side lines of Clothing Issue.

Once an inmate came in to get his shoes which had been left for repair. An altercation arose between him and Paddy which grew hotter and hotter until a fight was clearly about to start, and with shoemaker's tools at hand it promised to be bloody. Our officer had let them go until the climax approached, then scissored over the rail with his long legs, and strode toward the pair roaring as he went. He settled the dispute quickly by ordering the visitor to take his shoes and get out. He did so, but not before snarling at Paddy, "You lousy double-crossing thief, I'll get you someday."

Paddy protested to the officer with pious unction that he had offered the inmate the right pair of shoes, but the latter had put on the whole show just to get something better.

"You're a damn liar," said the officer, "but I'm not going to have my department all bloodied up."

Later when the officer was out of the room I could hear the shoemaker give his side of the story and his opinion of the inmate: "That cheap son-of-a-bitch never gives you nothing! A guy in J block gives me a carton to switch his shoes for a better pair—he's a regular guy—and when I say I'll switch, I switch. My word is good. If I get paid, I deliver. That's business. Now Reds there, he's different—he's just a swindler at heart." Paddy was talking about my enemy who

101

worked in the cage where clothing for released prisoners was kept. "Now what does Reds do—he's got the neatest racket in this place. He's dealing with guys who can hear only one thing, the sweetest song they ever heard, 'I'm going out, I'm going out.'"

A strained voice broke in: "Quit it, quit it, I can't take it. You'll have me blowing my top."

And another: "Maybe they've got Janes waiting for them outside."

Then Paddy again: "Well, these guys've looked at blue suits so long they never want to see one again. They take the appetite away. So they make a deal with Reds—two cartons for a gray-and-black-check suit and a pair of honest-to-god outside shoes, and they pay in advance. What does Reds give 'em? Heh! An oversized pale blue suit that fits like a wrapper and a pair of shoes that any wise guy could spot as prison issue at fifty paces. If one of these guys squawks, Reds chills him: 'One more beef out of you, buddy, and you get some more free board and lodging.' And they shut up—everybody thinks Reds has an underground to the warden."

"In a pig's eye he has," said someone.

"Well, he acts like it, and no one takes the chance. They're all thinking how they'd like to carve Reds' heart out and bite it, only then they wouldn't need no going-away suit at all."

"With the Janes waiting outside," came a voice.

"Quit it," said another. "Stop talking about Janes. It gives me goose pimples."

Paddy again: "Anyway, Reds gets away with it. What a racket! Now with me it's different—when I make a deal it's a deal."

This conversation had been carried on loudly and blithely despite the fact that Reds could hear it as well as I; the epithets applied to him were much stronger than I have set down here, but if they hurt him he didn't show it, nor did he reply. In fact, he gave the impression that the conversation flattered him somewhat. The comments did homage to his superior cleverness, which was the quality upon which he most prided himself. He was confident that he could outwit anybody. He considered his presence in jail as just one of those things—the best of fielders are perfect for a hundred chances and then the ball takes a funny hop and an error is marked up against him. The only man who never makes an error is the one who never takes a chance.

When Reds' customers came in to get their going-away outfits, Clothing Issue was stimulated by thoughts of the outside world. Dozens of questions were asked: "Where you going, buddy? What've you got to do?" And, as might be expected, there was plenty of talk about women: "Dated up for the first night? What does she look like? Take me along in your pocket, won't you, buddy? Just for one night, then ship me back parcel post."

The thought of going out created intense nervous excitement. Outside might actually be a terribly dull place, but it was outside nevertheless, and it drew the prisoners' minds ceaselessly like a magnet.

Among our visitors was often the Top Man of H-2. He was in charge of the laundry, also located in the basement, next door to Clothing Issue. He would come in, tall, his head up, and carrying an impressive air. He had a greeting for everyone. How eager they all were to call him by his nickname! He would have business with one or more of us, most frequently with Reds, which was conducted in low tones and with dispatch. Then, with a wave of his hand intended for everyone in the room, he was gone, leaving a residue of lively conversation—what a good guy he was, always ready to do a favor; a good man to deal with, and a good man to go to for help. A speaker would draw attention to himself by asserting he had known him on the outside. Another would assert that he had a friend who knew him. Both connections would be good for an anecdote. All the comments highlighted certain humane and delightful qualities of the Top Man, but left his morals in utter obscurity. Apparently he had lived in a shadowy world where law and morality relaxed and became "hail fellow."

Three weeks or more passed in this depressing place before my redheaded enemy across the way spoke to me. The officer was out when it happened. He came across the passageway and stood opposite my desk and said, "I have a proposition to make. We can be friends." I replied that I knew of no reason why we shouldn't be friends. He sat on the edge of my desk, one foot on the floor and the other swinging loosely in the air, and unfolded his proposition:

"There's a guy in F-block who wants a pair of shoes, soft leather and lightweight. His feet are killing him. He's good for two cartons if the deal goes through."

I asked for the man's name and got his folder from the file. "He's not entitled to a new pair of shoes," I said.

"That's where you come in. You make the entry for a requisition. This is just one deal, and we can make a lot more like it."

"No," I answered, and put the folder away. "Nevertheless, I still see no reason for our being enemies."

He walked away without replying, and we did not speak again for many months.

As the weather outside grew cooler and the basement became more uncomfortable, the complaints became loud and sustained. Everyone in command of the jail from the warden down was condemned to a fate even more terrible than that of working in Clothing Issue. Even so, I noted that there was still considerable agreement on the fact that by and large Clothing Issue was a pretty cushy spot. You could loaf on the job and the "take" was good. But to me the spirit of the place was sickening. It seemed completely unreal, but there were times when I would wonder if this was really life and what I had known outside was an impossible dream.

The dormitory in H-3 offered little relief. It continued to be vile, but there were changes. The young Italian had gone to another cell block; the Kid had been given permission to move to the vacated cot next to mine, and the Swede made a habit of joining him to debate with me many things—particularly, of course, their own convictions. They had both read a great deal and pondered what they read. To me their judgment might have seemed immature, but they were sure of their judgment, as only the young can be sure.

The first night the Kid occupied the cot next to mine after the lights had been dimmed, he asked me rather hesitantly if I would pray with him. He knew and I knew that doing so would be an ordeal, but we prayed under a volley of ribald remarks and of objects more tangible than words. Above the racket I could hear the voice of my young friend. There was no ostentation about it, only a compelling sincerity. He prayed for all men and he prayed for those about him, and through his prayer ran the unspoken appeal, "May God have mercy upon them, for they know not what they do." I was relieved when it was over, but I was touched to the point where I had to swallow a sob. He seemed so young, only a few years older than my own son, and he had committed himself to this torment. Perhaps he was wrong, but who am I to say? I had an affection for him and could not let him down.

We prayed each night thereafter for several months until he left the dormitory. The assaults upon us lessened as time went on and finally ceased. Perhaps the challenge to the wit of the dormitory had lost its zest. Perhaps, as I hoped, the young fellow's sincerity had compelled a reluctant respect.

There were other changes. My other neighbor, known as the Rabbit, who had at first kept his back to me, began taking quick glances at me out of the corners of his eyes; then he looked full upon me, and at the end of a week or more he spoke. Once the ice was broken he became eagerly talkative. He was, I judge, about sixty years of age, a Jew who had conducted a highly successful business in some phase of finance. His present plight, as I understood his long and involved story, arose from a lack of comprehension by the Department of Justice of the intricacies of high finance. The attitude of the government was a great mistake. I nodded assent. There may have been a flaw in his argument but I certainly could not have pointed it out.

As the young Italian had prophesied, I was soon looking at his photographs. The first was a picture of a trim yacht. Then came one of himself at the wheel, then a series of group pictures. He would point to himself in a white yachting costume and name his guests. He seemed to think I should recognize the names. I presumed they were men of wealth and prominence in the financial world, but they were out of my realm. He had pictures taken in many harbors along the Atlantic coast and in the West Indies. As he showed and explained them, he forgot the present and lived again in those glorious days.

I soon became acquainted with another of the Rabbit's idiosyncrasies. He insisted on bribing the prisoners who served our food in the dining room in order to get toast and extra supplies of sugar. Sometimes he would conceal these items on his person to bring them back to the dormitory, and every once in a while he was detected by the guards who watched us vigilantly at mealtime. Then he was ordered out of line as we marched out of the dining room, to the great amusement of the other prisoners. Our quarters were occasionally searched without warning for contraband, and he was usually caught with odd items of the illegal food. For his violations of the rules he had to go through a hearing, a reprimand, and a deprivation of privileges, which would ultimately be restored. I doubt if his urge to take food was altogether appetite. He always seemed to feel that he had to prove to himself that he was not an ordinary person—he had to engage in a game of outwitting the adversary. In any event, it was a habit that was never broken.

It was in the dining room that I learned the source of his nickname. There was a rule that each prisoner must eat whatever he took away from the servers' table. Even so, the Rabbit's plate was usually piled higher than most. He liked to eat. He would sit on the edge of his bench, hunched over the table, his short legs barely touching the floor, and eat with concentration and purpose, for he had but twenty minutes. His lower jaw moved rapidly like that of a rabbit nibbling. Someone noticed the resemblance and the title stuck.

The White-Slaver, who was the chief performer in the coarse talk that went on after the lights were dimmed, had a cot some distance from mine. For a time after my arrival he could be counted on to make slurring remarks intended for my ears. When we passed each other he had a mocking expression on his face. Later on, his attitude seemed to change somewhat and he began nodding to me as we passed; ultimately we spoke and at times talked together at some length.

He told me, "Don't think I rode you because of that redheaded kike. I just don't like Christers—they stink. But I watched you, and you play your game all right. It's not my game and I ain't playing it. I like myself as I am. When I'm spilling dirt I like it. I'm here because I stubbed my toe and got grabbed, but when I get out of this hole I'm sure going to be hot—the bastards ain't going to get me again."

In reply I said that I merely acted as I thought it was willed I should. He looked at me sharply, but let it pass. We got along well enough thereafter.

There was a difference of opinion about ventilation in the dormitory which was a cause of dissension. The younger men put on a show of toughness and insisted on keeping the windows open at night. They bullied anybody who challenged them. This became a hardship as the weather grew colder. Sometimes the snow drifted in on the bedcovers and made little mounds on the floor.

It was in December, I believe, that a stooped little fellow came in carrying his bundle. His cot was across the passageway from mine. His reputation had preceded him to prison, for he was a prominent figure in the moving-picture world. Everybody knew about him. He was as withered and fragile as a dried leaf and fumbled ineptly at the simple task of making his bed. When I spoke a word of greeting to him he seemed startled. After the lights were dimmed and the windows opened, the cold wind drove him hurriedly under his blankets where I watched him move restlessly. He shivered, and his teeth chattered. He was unable to keep warm. I called to him across the passageway and asked him how he felt. He muttered something about diabetes and how cold he was. I offered him one of my blankets, and he accepted it. Then I tucked him in and suggested, since he was bald, that he put a towel over his head, but even then the chill seemed to reach into his bones. Finally I saw the little figure bowed down under a bundle of bedclothes making his way to the washroom, which was heated, where he curled himself up on the floor. The guard routed him out of there, and the next day he was given a hearing for violation of the rules and was transferred to other quarters. I met him later as an aide in the library.

The problem of keeping the windows open or shut created

such contention that the guard heard about it and undertook to settle the matter. He secured an independent opinion from the doctor as to how many windows should be opened for proper ventilation and gave his orders accordingly, warning that if they were not complied with the whole dormitory would be penalized by loss of privileges—no cards, no chess, no checkers, and no stockade.

He was a good officer, careful in the performance of his duties and playing no favorites. He tried to obtain obedience by reasonable means before he turned anyone in. I came to know him rather intimately. His parents were German and had come to this country before he was born, but his mother still wrote to him in German script which he had difficulty reading so he called upon me for help. When later I moved to other quarters he expressed regret at my going and told me that my influence had helped to maintain order in the dormitory. We both knew that the place had quieted down and that many of the men seemed to like to talk their troubles over with me, but we also knew that the White-Slaver had left a month or more before my departure—probably the prime reason for the new peacefulness.

Not long after I left H-3 the guard was transferred to Alcatraz just in time for the famous insurrection. He was the first man to be killed. The story was picked up by our jail and repeated again and again. My friend had been caught on an upper tier of cells when the break came. His attackers were armed, and they crowded him to the rail around a rotunda and demanded his keys at the point of a gun. He drew them out and tossed them over the rail to the floor three stories below. They shot him and pitched his body after the keys. The gesture he made would be like him. It was a bunch of keys against his life, but the keys were the symbol of his duty and he acted the only part he knew. I honor him for it and salute him.

11.

THE TOP MAN

On Sundays there were no work assignments except in the hospital and kitchen. To some of the men the day was an aching void; they were thrown on their own resources, and they had none. The wound they had suffered when they were cut off from the world asserted itself and throbbed painfully. The restless uncertainty that pervades a jail was exaggerated, and little relief was derived from the church services held in the auditorium over the dining room—the Roman Catholic in the morning, and the Protestant in the evening. The Jews held theirs on Saturdays before the weekly movie was shown.

I always kept busy on Sunday writing the weekly letter to my wife. In doing so I gave full rein to my emotions, then slowed them down to a walk as they reached the point of my pencil. In addition I read, and I talked to many of my fellows who sought relief from their uneasiness by unburdening themselves to me. I attended church services but, I must confess, not regularly. They were reminders of something my mind tried to close off, and I found them a source of unhappiness rather than consolation.

More time was granted us in stockade than on weekdays. I remember one Sunday—it was late in the season for outdoor stockade, perhaps our last until spring, but it was a soft warm day with a vague mystery in the air. There were upwards of a thousand of us milling about, the hard-packed earth under our feet, with the walls about us, and the misty blue sky above.

The gallery of faces familiar to me had grown considerably since I had left quarantine, but it was still limited to a small section of the population—and I was feeling none too sociable that afternoon—so for a time I walked alone. I could see the Baron taking his exercise with quick strides, heel-and-toe, to stay within the ban on running. I wondered how he had progressed with his complaints to the warden. And there was the Top Man of H-2, walking tall with measured steps. The man called Blackie the Clerk on his left and the one called the Red Slugger on his right accompanied him like body-guards. He held informal court with those who wished to interview him.

I saw my enemy Reds holding quick, earnest conversations with one person and another. I noticed a number of men I knew by reputation only. Young Dago Blackie, Italian both in looks and name, was always the center of a group. On the outside his rackets had been manifold, including the one that tripped him up, stealing automobiles; on the inside, he managed a gang that sold "protection" for a carton or so of cigarettes a week. He had a rival, a big fellow from the hard-coal country known as the Polak, who also sold protection. If you bought from them, nothing would happen to you. If you did not buy, the chances were you would find your life made miserable, and you might even meet with an unavoidable accident.

There was a fellow called the Manager, a quiet, efficient sort of chap, whose work assignment put him in charge of the officers' mess. He appeared in general stockade only on Sundays. He was doing twenty-five years for holding up a mail truck and therefore lived in the long-termers' block, B-3. A group was always gathered about him, for he managed the

111

baseball teams which played during the summer in the evenings between six and eight. Plans were under way (with the administration's approval) to lay out a diamond in stockade and build a grandstand with lumber to be purchased out of the prisoners' commissary profits. Population still had to be induced to approve of the expenditure, and the Manager was campaigning. In this group was usually a tall, lanky man who had operated a still in the Tennessee mountains, rather an irresolute chap who became purposeful and alive when he had a baseball in his hand. He was a natural athlete and batted, fielded, and pitched with easy grace. Population admired him greatly. In the group I could also see the team's assistant manager, a great hulk of a man topping six feet four and possessing an ample girth. He weighed almost three hundred pounds. Two men had been killed at the time he was captured, and he was doing a life term. He lived in B-3 with the Manager. Population named him the Killer.

There was another resident of that block who attracted my attention. Something in his powerful build, his granite jaw, and forbidding expression suggested a great machine, and he was known as the Army Tank. The likeness was heightened by the way he walked back and forth alone; there was power and weight in him, as if he would crush whatever got in his way. He was said to be curt with others. He might speak a few words of greeting, but like as not he would look you full in the face and then say after a pause, "I don't like your looks. Keep out of my way," and nobody defied him. We had spoken words of greeting to each other on several occasions, and I had not as yet been dismissed.

I noticed the Swede with his pale hair and face and his strained eyes. He was with a group of conscientious objectors, where the Kid, more rugged in build and more somber, could also be seen. Taken as a group they were clean-cut young

112

men preoccupied with something they could see and which they felt the world overlooked. Not far from them were Jehovah's Witnesses gathered about one of their number who was reading the Bible.

In another part of the stockade was the man they called Irish. How he got his nickname I never knew, for he was of German descent. Everybody in jail knew him as the prisoner in charge of the pharmacy, a post that held as much prestige as any other work assignment. He carried himself as a man of importance should, walking with the strut of a regular army sergeant, his head thrown back and his chin pulled in. Many came up to interview him. He never broke stride, and disposed of their inquiries brusquely.

One grouping apparent in stockade was that between white and colored prisoners. The line between them was not fixed, but it could be clearly noted where the one group faded out and the other began. By common consent they stayed apart, and both discountenanced any intermingling.

The gallery of faces and personalities was absorbingly interesting. I was interrupted in my contemplation of it by the Postmaster, who came up to me with his crippled walk. As we moved along we gossiped of our respective duties and of our acquaintances in H-3 and elsewhere. Presently we were on the subject that had the strongest attraction—the people of the outside world from whom we had been cut off. He talked eagerly of the latest news of his wife and daughter. It was encouraging news. His daughter could walk again, though with difficulty. She was working hard and was proud of her improvement. He was proud too. Then, before he could stop himself, he was talking of the time when he would be eligible for parole, only eight months hence.

He checked himself in some confusion, for he knew that my sentence was ten years and my parole date must have seemed an interminable time away. I didn't tell him that I had resolved against accepting parole, for a parolee was required to sign an agreement containing many conditions which seemed to me to constitute a confession of guilt. The light that shone in his eyes when he spoke of his possible release was a little hard to bear, but it thrilled him so much to think of it that I myself brought the subject back into our discussion.

He moved on. I was alone again when I encountered the Army Tank. He spoke a greeting, and then, as if he had made up his mind abruptly, he stopped to talk to me. His first remark was, "I've followed your case, Reverend, and you should not be here." It was a gratifying opening which led to a brief review of my case and then of his, equally brief. His was seven years old. I had heard gossip about it; its outlines were vague and a bit fantastic. He had been employed, I suppose as some sort of "private eye," to recover some letters from a young woman. They must have been highly embarrassing letters. He recovered them, but in the process violated some federal laws. Apparently the violations were serious and readily provable. He pleaded guilty, but would say nothing more. His sentence was twenty years.

What he wanted to talk to me about was something quite different. His son was studying for the ministry in the Moravian church, to which his family belonged. What the Army Tank wanted of me was to learn about the ministry as a calling, for he had become intensely interested in the subject. His own mishap had had a major influence on his son's decision, and he felt a degree of responsibility for it.

He told me ruefully, "I guess it'll make no difference what I think of his choice—if he makes up his mind it sets like concrete. He's too much like me that way, but he's a good kid—stands by his mother and comes up here to see me with her. We were kind of pals in the old days, and he's not turning his back on me now."

I tried to tell him something of both the trials and the compensations of the ministry, and I summed up by saying that if his son had a sincere concept of the spiritual quality of the Christian faith and an unaffected liking for his fellow men, which would give him the natural desire to help them in their aspirations and their daily troubles, his life would be a full one and he would never have the time or inclination to regret his choice.

The Army Tank listened attentively and after a pause said, "I'd like you to read some of his letters. You'll know him better then." I could tell that he was proud of the letters. He went on, "I'm eligible for parole and want to get out. My record is all right. I've got a good work assignment as clerk to the associate warden. It keeps me pretty much apart from population, and I'm going to keep my nose clean. Maybe I can help him then, but if I find I'm standing in his way I'll just fade out and watch him from a distance."

Our conversation ended when my companion had to return to his duties, and once more I was left to myself. Strolling past the little group surrounding the Top Man, I became interested in what was going on. A young fellow was telling his troubles in a high-pitched voice which seemed on the verge of hysterical sobbing. I had seen him on the ball field. He was from Georgia and the inmates called him "the Cracker." I could get just enough of his story to realize that some conditions he faced were simply too much to bear. Then he broke down. I heard him repeating, "I gotta do something. I gotta do something." The Top Man had been listening gravely, and when the outburst had run its course he put his hand on the young fellow's shoulder and smiled. It was a reassuring gesture.

"Now just a moment, just a moment." His deep voice was soothing. "Let's think this over. Those walls over there have got us all, and it's no use bucking them. We can run our heads against them, but they'll still be there. It's only our heads that'll get hurt, but someday those walls will fade out. Easy does it."

Then he tackled the particular trouble. It was nothing special—like so many problems that afflict a jail, it may seem minor on the surface but it produces frictions that chafe and chafe until a raw spot appears and men are driven mad. But as the Top Man analyzed the trouble, it did not seem so bad. Then he suggested something that might ease the problem. "I think that can be done," he said, and he was believed.

The Cracker went away calmed down. When the Top Man said a thing could be done, there was faith that it would be done—a justified faith, for the guards were always pleased to work with him. He could do favors for them on the outside and help them with their duties on the inside. His hints about advisable adjustments in prison routine were quickly brought to the attention of the administration, and usually they were acted upon. More than once he had headed off trouble among the prisoners. Perhaps he supported outward order instinctively for his own comfort, but he also took a genuine interest in his fellow inmates and tried to guard them against their own desperate folly.

He saw me standing near by, and when the young Georgian left him he came over and walked alongside me. I liked to talk to him; there was charm in his conversation. And I think he liked to talk to me, for he could give free expression to ideas. Perhaps I was even the foil which gave rise to those ideas. As we walked, Blackie the Clerk and the Red Slugger, the "bodyguards," dropped back a pace, and the other inmates let us alone. "The Top Man has invited the Reverend to walk with him," and it raised my prestige in population several notches.

I asked him if he could help the Cracker.

"I think so," he said. "The remedy is simple and, I have

no doubt, will be applied. The Cracker's a good chap, but emotional. You can see he's strong and fast, and if he blew his top there might be a lot of damage done before he was stopped. And he wouldn't be nice to look at when the guards got through working on him.

"There are a lot of interesting fellows here," he went on. "I wonder why so many people read novels filled with second-hand characters when there is so much firsthand material all around us. Take my clerk, Blackie—he's a small-time rack-eteer. They got him for counterfeiting O.P.A. stamps. He'll never be anything but small-time, even though he has big ideas. When he came into H-2 he was sullen and defiant, always watching for a chance to get even with . . . nobody in particular, just everybody. He was headed for trouble and maybe Alcatraz. But he got attached to me, and I use him to keep track of my affairs. I give him his commissary money, and he feels like a big shot."

Each prisoner was entitled to receive a maximum of ten dollars a month from the outside to be spent in the commis-sary. Some got nothing. As population knew, the Top Man received considerably more than ten dollars. The method he used to get additional funds called for the co-operation of several other inmates. Nobody ever "squealed," for he was liberal with both his money and his cigarettes. He always had a supply of cigarettes in excess of what was permitted any one prisoner, and as a precaution against a sudden search he "banked" them in a number of different lockers. A clerk was useful in keeping a record of his loans, his gifts, and his assets.

"My other handyman, the Red Slugger," he went on, "used to be a welterweight fighter. He always had managers who made a practice of overmatching him. At his best he was no more than a fair fighter, and they fed him to better men. He was slow and made them look good, but he took plenty of punishment. Now he's a bit punchy. His last manager managed him right into the Pen and managed to keep himself out.

"There was nothing intricate about the Slugger's offense. He was a strong-arm guy riding a truckload of contraband liquor. When he got here I must have looked like a manager to him, so he adopted me. As long as he's living in H-2 I can keep an eye on him, but there are some men in F-block who keep urging him to join them. They want a champion for their faction. They pour flattery on him thick as molasses and he eats it all up. He's proud of his muscles, and they make a big fuss about them, so he swells his muscles and struts around as chesty as a cock. Maybe they'll get him. If he wants to go I won't stop him, but I wager he'll be stepping into trouble."

We walked in silence a few moments; then he nodded his head:

"Look over there."

I obeyed and saw the Red Slugger surrounded by an eager circle. I saw him lunge at the air with his fist.

"There he is," said the Top Man. "He slipped away when I joined up with you. He's telling them how he knocked some guy kicking. He can still feel the thrill of that punch at the end of his mitt. He's forgotten the times he was on the receiving end. I suspect he'll be moving to F-block soon, and I'll need a new bodyguard. Anyway, you can see what I mean. I know enough about my two men to tell their stories from the time they were born. I don't know what'll happen to them in the next chapter, but I can speculate."

The conversation shifted to another inmate.

"I notice you've been talking to the Army Tank," he said. "It's not many that do. He speaks to me when we meet, but that's all. I've managed to piece together his story, and you won't find a better one in any book. Did he tell you why he's here?"

"Yes," I said, "in a general way. I have some idea of what

it was all about by adding what he told me to what I had heard before."

"I knew about it at the time it happened," said my companion, "and I know the girl at the bottom of it. She's a good-looking little cat, smart as paint and hard as nails. By the way, the Tank must have made up his mind about you some time ago. He's told both Dago Blackie and the Polak to 'lay off the Reverend.'"

"That doesn't sound like him," I protested. "He told me he was keeping his nose clean so he can make parole."

"All the inmates know that too, but he has a way of saying things that makes you believe them. Both of those men are tough and dangerous, but I wouldn't expect them to bother you. Nobody wants to tangle with the Tank. That's the way it is—a strong man can get what he wants without fighting for it. He's never asked a favor of me or given me his confidence. What did he talk about with you?"

I replied, "He spoke to me mostly of his family, and though he never asked me to keep it confidential, I'm sure he understood I would."

My companion nodded. "Quite right. He's not one who asks for sympathy, and he wouldn't want his feelings blabbed about."

Our discussion turned to myself. He asked me how I was making out, and I told him frankly that I was living a strange, nightmarish existence, but I was asking neither sympathy nor help and didn't expect to ask any.

"Quite right," he said again. "Don't let those rats think they've gotten to you. You'll get a break. Incidentally, I hear that Clothing Issue is a cushy job, and I've been told you were offered a chance to get into business on a fair division of profits—fifty-fifty—and you were too snooty to accept the offer. A little deal now and then might lessen the monotony and help you get along."

" 'Snooty,' " I said, "may not be the appropriate adjective; 'stupid' might be better. If I tried that business, I'm certain I would make a fearful mess of it."

He looked at me and smiled. "I wouldn't use either adjective," he said. "I'd say you're playing the game the way you're built to play it. And that's a good rule to follow. The worst flops I've ever seen are the people who try to play someone else's game. Then too, you're a minister, and the boys are watching you. They don't like ministers, and if they found a rotten spot you'd need protection."

After a pause he added, "I'll let you in on something. I was asked to use my influence to soften you up. I'm not telling you who asked me. Guessing is your business. But I'll say, 'Nothing doing,' with my wholehearted support for your stand."

He seemed somewhat thoughtful for a moment, then spoke again: "My father was a minister. I can see him now. He had high cheekbones and forehead, and a long, gaunt face. His eyes looked out at you from deep sockets. You know the breed—I think they have the finest faces in the world. He was dedicated to self-denial, and he did only the hardest and most thankless tasks. How he begot me is beyond understanding. I sacked all his precepts. He knew it and forgave me, but he couldn't forgive himself for forgiving. He's gone now. I have him mounted on a pedestal in my mind. I bow to him, and then, as I always did, I go my own way. But don't think I regret not following in his footsteps. What a shuffling fool I would have been if I had tried!"

There was a considerable break in the conversation; at last he went on: "Each of us has an image of himself in his own mind, and that's what he plays up to. That's himself. There was a man I knew who fought a thousand battles to get a place and hold onto it in the unstable medium we call society.

I never knew a more magnificent egotist. As he grew in importance his own image of himself grew until it looked like the great Khan. And he saw it so vividly that he made others see it.

"Then he fought his last fight and was outflanked by the government. Income tax caught up with him, just as with me. He knew the traps—as I did—but he despised them as being set for little creatures; nobody could ever spring them on him. But his enemies managed to spring them just the same, and he was caught, just as I was caught, only I wasn't so big. They brought him to Lewisburg. When I came here and saw him, the mighty figure of the Earth Shaker had disappeared and in its place was just a shriveled little old man with a vacant stare getting pushed around in population. His image of himself had been wrecked. They took him out to die, but he had died with his image long before they buried him.

"So you can see how I carry on here. It's a small pattern of what I did on the outside, but it keeps my image on its pedestal. I'm still myself. It explains a lot of things that go on around us—the deals paid off in cigarettes, the trickery, the thieving, the striving for slightly different clothing, shoes, or belt buckles, the swaggering of gang leaders, the quirks of the conscientious objectors, the desperate plans for escape, the violence of race hates, and the screaming patriotism. How absurd they all seem here, and yet how vital they are to the preservation of each man's ego! Some there are who seem to cover up their image. They reduce themselves to nothingness and do their time in a coma, but I would fear that more than death."

As I listened I could understand why the Top Man had been considered good magazine copy when he was still listed among the near-great in the outside world.

12.

MEN IN WHITE

It was December, and Christmas in jail was at hand. The day and season were always celebrated extensively both in my family and my church, and I associated them with lights and brightness; now their approach only deepened the darkness of the way ahead. The only light came from the intermittent visits of my wife, from her letters, and from the far-off beacon of my appeal, which I dared not concentrate on for fear that if it were snuffed out the darkness would become overwhelming.

Shortly before Christmas I was visited in Clothing Issue by the acting chaplain of the prison. He was the minister of a church in Lewisburg and had taken over prison visitations only until the vacant post could be filled. He was an earnest young fellow whittled too fine to be tough, and I saw him wince at the conversation and the atmosphere of the place. Later he visited me again, this time in the dormitory, but he found it no better than Clothing Issue. The visit took place late in the afternoon. The Swede had returned from the hospital at the end of his shift and was sprawled on his cot in a fitful sleep. Suddenly he awoke with a stabbing, agonizing cry. My visitor was much affected. He stammered his excuses and left. The fellow was too senstive to the sufferings of others to endure being chaplain of a jail, but he had the qualifications of humility and of human sympathy which some ministers lack.

Other ministers visited us, and one of them, a Protestant,

appeared in full vestments encasing his sweetly rounded paunch upon which rested a gold crucifix hung on a gold chain. The crucifix rose and fell softly as he breathed. He carried a prayer book, and his voice intoned his greetings and his commiserations. His attitude seemed to say, "You poor misguided wretches. How you should appreciate the blessings of the church and of God which I bring you!"

There was a Catholic priest, too, and he wore a smile with his vestments as he scattered pronouncements about him: "Be of Good Cheer. Keep Your Spirits High. All Will Be Well." He flung these phrases about as one might sow grass seed. They were mockeries to men faced with bitter reality.

I shall never again assume, as I once did, that a prison chaplain may be casually chosen from among those who do not fit into the normal functions of the church.

The young acting chaplain was interested enough in my situation to urge that I ask for an assignment to other work than that in Clothing Issue. When I refused, he went to the warden himself, and shortly afterward I was called to the office of the assistant to the associate warden and was told that I had been assigned to the hospital surgical ward as a nurse and should report the following morning at seven. I was satisfied to leave Clothing Issue, but I had learned something about a nurse's job when I was trustee of a hospital, and I did not expect my new work to be either easy or cheering.

It was at least fifteen minutes before seven the next morning when I entered the main corridors, an hour before prison industries would stir into action. The central highway of the prison looked long and hollow and deserted. I showed my pass midway along its length at the captain's desk and again when I entered the first floor of the hospital.

The surgical ward was on the third floor. The elevator was

123

not for the use of inmates, so I walked up three flights. To my right as I entered the ward's central hallway was the desk of the captain of nurses. I swung around to face a short, stout woman in a white dress and with a white cap pressed down on her gray hair. She had a face and voice that made me feel as if I were in the presence of a top sergeant. The pince-nez glasses she wore glittered at me. I handed her my pass. She did not look at it.

"So you're the Lutheran minister!" She punctuated her statement with a sniff.

I assented.

"You're a political prisoner?" Again she sniffed, and again I agreed.

"I've been in the Navy most of my life and in jails for almost ten years. I've seen politics in both places, and I don't like politics." Once more she sniffed.

I was not sure whether her dislike of politics meant that she did not like me or just that she did not like my case. I stood mute.

"You will report back here to me at eight o'clock and then go to the laundry issue for a white uniform. You will now report to the head nurse at his office down the corridor, last door on your left."

As she made this statement she closed her right eye. I was startled. Fortunately, as I later learned, I did not respond in kind. In the head nurse's office I was greeted pleasantly enough by three young men in white. They noticed my interest in a rack of charts, each bearing the name and number of a patient, and the head nurse, tallest of the three, explained, "They're our own work. Not bad, if you ask me. It's a little trick you'll learn quickly."

He spoke to the others: "One of you guys give him a leaflet of instructions on how to become a nurse in three easy lessons." I was given one.

A moment later the Swede entered and introduced me to the dark-haired young fellow who followed him and who was greeted by the other nurses as "Johnnie." The Swede gave me a warm welcome and assured everyone that I was a good friend of his and could use their help. The conversation then became general, and it was full of airy allusions to the nurses' work. Before long Johnnie was giving an admirable imitation of Madam Captain.

Suddenly I saw his expression change with extraordinary rapidity from mockery to sober concern, and he asked to be shown the chart of a certain new patient. I turned and saw Madam Captain in the doorway.

"Johnnie," she said sharply, "if I catch you at that again, I'll see that you do a stretch on the coal pile."

Johnnie looked at her with a gravely troubled expression. "Now Madam Captain, what can you mean?"

"You know perfectly well what I mean."

For a moment I thought a smile was going to break the grimness of her face, but it got no further than her eyes.

"Johnnie," she said, "you're a complete liar. Now go back where you belong." She turned to the Swede. "And you too."

Johnnie and the Swede started for the door, but Johnnie turned as he went out and said goodbye to the other nurses—and as he did so, he closed his right eye.

"Johnnie," snapped the Captain, "stop that nonsense."

Her back was turned to him. She could not possibly have seen what he was doing, but she seemed to know anyway. After they left, she followed them.

"Round number ninety-nine," the head nurse announced. "No blows struck, no knockdowns, and nobody hurt."

Then the others began to talk about Johnnie. He and the Swede were attendants—and very good ones— in the operating room. While he was working, Johnnie was serious. He never lost his head, anticipating the surgeons' needs quickly and deftly, and his services were highly regarded. Otherwise, however, he was impishly irresponsible and the delight of the ward. He was doing two years for liquor violation in North Carolina. "He's a clever thief," said someone. "He's the only man in this ward who can steal supplies and get away with it."

Another said, "That's right. The other day he snitched aspirin tablets from the Captain's emergency supply. I don't know how he did it. But she knew they were missing—I'll bet she counts them every day—and she knew just where to go. She didn't have any proof, and Johnnie gave her that look of injured innocence, but she told him, 'Johnnie, you're a complete liar. I'm warning you, if I catch your fingers in my aspirin bottle, I'll break every one of them.'"

Someone else explained for my benefit, "Aspirin has a high value out in population, you know. Two or three tablets in a cup of coffee will give you pleasant dreams."

After a while the three nurses went on duty, and I was left alone. I turned to the window and looked out on the same view I had seen from my quarantine cell in late September. Then the hills had been clothed in the rich colors of autumn; now they were stark and desolate, but there was grandeur in their desolation. I gazed at them for a long time, then sat down on a steel chair and remembered the leaflet. In my next letter to my wife I recited its criteria for good nurses which appeared under the heading, "Essentials for Success in Nursing": "Desire to help the unfortunate," "Conscientiousness," "Courtesy," "Dignity," "Sympathy and self-control," "Unselfishness," "Giving a kindly greeting to one admitted to the ward," "When your patient seems worried, try to find the cause without being curious." I added one more personal admonition in the letter: "May I not be found wanting."

Shortly after eight o'clock I presented myself at the laundry, where the Top Man was the inmate in charge. He was pleased to see to it that I got a properly fitting uniform, and he told me that he felt my new assignment was definitely a rung up the ladder for me.

Marching back along the corridor in freshly laundered white shirt, jacket, and trousers, I was conscious of the change from my dull blue suit. Clothes and color can affect a man's spirit. Besides, the uniform typified a definite change of atmosphere from my previous employment. The hospital was governed by the Public Health Service, not by the Department of Justice. It functioned not under, but in co-ordination with, the warden of the prison. The hospital Chief, a man of medium size with a fine open face, was every inch a doctor. To him the hospital was a medical center, no more or no less. The fact that its patients were inmates of a jail was a factor of no material significance to him; nor was he concerned with the prisoner status of the aides, but treated them with dignity and respect and received respect in return.

The regular hospital staff consisted of six doctors, including a psychologist, a psychiatrist, and the two surgeons in our ward. There were in addition one inmate doctor and two staff dentists. The staff doctors wore uniforms similar to those used in the Navy, and the Chief's rank corresponded with that of a commander. The first surgeon—technically, a surgical officer—was second in command. He was a stalwart fellow with a prominent nose and a fierce temper. He was one of those who had caused me so much suffering when I went through the "gauntlet" at the time of my admission to the jail. The second surgical officer was tall, well poised, and politely impersonal.

The dominating personality of the surgical ward was Madam Captain. Her presence was always felt. She had as many eyes as Argus, and nothing escaped her. She ruled the place. The janitor, a little colored fellow called Boots, was kept eternally busy cleaning and polishing a spot here and a spot there which called for cleaning or polishing, and the immaculately clean ward gave evidence of his efforts. Madam Captain made visitations to the rooms, to the open ward, and to the sun porch, and knew every one of the continually incoming and outgoing patients. Frequently she brought her assistant with her, a middle-aged woman none too alluring. But they were women nonetheless and thus were subjected often to coarsely suggestive remarks which were meant to be jocular. She offered no rejoinder until certain boundaries fixed by herself had been crossed. Then she shut off all comments with a vigor that was indisputable.

She was cursed pretty freely behind her back, and there was much sly mimicking of her peculiarities—not only her sniffing and winking, but also her chuckles, of which she gave exactly three to show mirth (only on the rarest occasions was a fourth added), and the slant of her normally stiffly erect cap when she was stormy. Nevertheless, there was an undertone of respect and even liking for her in the ward.

After work she returned to her home in the city of Lewisburg. Once, later on, I was given a report on her life in that far-off world by a doctor who had seen her at a women's meeting. He told me that he did not recognize her at first, she seemed so modest and reserved. Her hair, which was done up in an aggressively militant fashion for us, nestled softly about her face, from which all the grimness had disappeared. She might have served as a model for motherliness.

The doctor also told me that the women at the meeting, knowing where she worked, asked her if she knew me, and when she said she did they were full of questions. A widely advertised Nazi spy was something to know about. "I don't know what they expected," said the doctor, "some sort of monster, I suppose, and when she told them rather shyly that you seemed to be a quiet sort of man, conscientious in your duties, and that she had no trouble with you at all, they were very much let down."

But this took place six or eight weeks after my arrival in surgery ward. At the beginning she was very distant to me, addressing me as little as possible and then curtly by my last name, and treating me as if I were a block of wood. I wouldn't say that she resented my presence, but she certainly made it clear that she was not giving me her stamp of approval.

I soon learned that I had at least one real enemy in the hospital. He was the inmate doctor, an able physician whose prison assignment was to work with the regular hospital staff. Population had a story of his reason for imprisonment which was almost too fantastic to believe. He was said to have been an intimate of Stalin who had maintained his connection with Moscow after he came to this country to live. He was charged with importing counterfeit money and was serving a long term. "Joe's Doctor" was the nickname he carried in recognition of his reputed friend, and he hated me as a Nazi although we had never met. He spread stories in the ward that I was a brutal Nazi working in Hitler's interest and would not hesitate to poison the whole jail. He warned everybody against me. Evidently he was a convincing talker, for he quite clearly turned the attitudes of some of the staff and patients against me.

Fortunately, these warnings appeared to be a matter of no concern to the Chief. He had a way of making up his own mind and then carrying out his plans without wasting time arguing about them. And I did not permit attacks upon my character to interfere with my earnest effort to learn the duties of a nurse. Most people know something about them, but there is a wide difference between doing them right and doing them half-right.

The charts of the patients were kept in the nurse's office. We learned to read them and to fill them out. We learned how to make beds for surgical and postoperative cases; how to use surgical gauze and to apply bandages; how to carry a patient from one bed to another; how to use the apparatus for sterilizing surgical instruments under steam and high pressure; how to give injections, intravenous, intramuscular, and subcutaneous; how to dress wounds; and, above all, how to be meticulous in observing the rules for cleanliness and sanitation.

I can remember Madam Captain repeating again and again with the monotonous regularity of a drill sergeant the cardinal principles of care and caution in giving medication: "Look three times before you give medicine to a patient. Look carefully at the prescription; note carefully the amount of the dose; look once more at the prescription when the medicine glass has been filled. Compare it again with the amount of the dose before you give it to the patient. Take nothing for granted. Look and check; look and check."

Once the nature of our duties were sufficiently mastered, a substantial amount of responsibility was imposed on the nurses. If one chose to do so he could do much to relieve suffering, either by direct methods or by providing little attentions to indicate interest and sympathy, which have a positive psychological effect.

Our patients were treated with individual care, and their meals, specially checked and prepared, were brought to them. After months or years of being a faceless number, the change was marked for a prisoner, and I could understand now why a stay in the hospital was considered something of a blessing. However, it was not long before I discovered that in the hospital as elsewhere business went on as usual, nurses receiving special payments for special services while those patients who had no commissary money got only casual attention.

There was a great demand for cigarettes by those who were capable of enjoying them. I had purchased a cigarette-making machine at the commissary which enabled me to be generous at a very low cost. I made no distinctions and received no fees. Some of the sufferers were appreciative, some were not. I remember one in particular, a military prisoner who had been convicted by court martial and sent back to us from his unit in North Africa. What his offense was I did not know. When I tended him, he cursed me for my pains and never relented, taking delight in calling me a Nazi and in expressing his opinion of all Nazis and Germans in the most violent language.

It was at times my duty to accompany the first surgeon in his visitations to the patients, carrying a number of items that he might need. In the early period of my training, I was still nothing but a number to him, but while we were tending the military prisoner, he joined in the attack upon the Nazis with a few bitter comments of his own. In the process it began to dawn on him who I was. On one occasion he spat in disgust, and I had to step back quickly to avoid it.

It must have been six or eight weeks after my new assignment began, that, while I was performing my duties for this patient—by no means pleasant ones—and was being reviled by him in his customary way, Madam Captain entered the room. She listened a moment and then turned on him.

"You're a surly dog. Somebody ought to break that big jaw of yours." To me she said, "Let him alone—he doesn't deserve decent treatment. He can wallow in his own dirt. He asked for it."

I shrugged my shoulders. "I am playing at being a doctor— a deputy doctor of a sort. It helps me to live with myself and to carry on. As for this fellow, he is just a medical case. What he says or what he thinks does not interest me."

She glittered at me for a moment, sniffed, and then walked on. I noticed my patient glaring at me. Thereafter he never seemed to get the same satisfaction out of insulting me.

Madam Captain too changed, no longer treating me as a creature without a brain, but assuming that I knew even more than I did. Her confidence in my medical knowledge was sometimes so great that it was difficult to live up to.

The difference of opinion among inmates concerning me gave rise to other incidents, one almost resulting in a tragedy. The Cracker from Georgia came into the hospital for a tonsilectomy, and after the operation came under my care in the ward. I found him to be a restless fellow impatient of the suffering he had to endure and disgusted with his confinement to a bed. He was doing himself no good. I did what I could to help him, and he appreciated it. He had a strong frame and long flat muscles that were pliant and supple, and I could sense his suppressed vitality. As it became easier for him to talk I learned more of his story. He, too, was a military prisoner, and he had not been in the army as a draftee much more than a month before he had trouble. Apparently a lot of things about army routine irked him, but he had been making an effort to comply with many rules he thought silly. Then along came a new officer he had not met before who stood him up before the other enlisted men and said things to him that "no white man would take."

The Cracker described what happened: "I let him have it. He sat down kind of hard, but he wasn't hurt much. He got up after a bit and walked off under his own power, but what a fuss they made about it—you might think I had killed the guy. And when they had me up before the court martial they wouldn't even listen to my side of the story; they just sent me up for five years for assault and battery on a superior officer. Now I ask you, is that fair?"

I had to smile at his naïve confusion. I knew something about how his offense looked from the other side of the table. But he went on:

"When I think what they done to me, something boils up

inside and I get mad clear through. Once I just went off my nut and started ramming around, but it done no good. I fetched up in the Hole for a couple of days, and that's no holiday. Now, when I'm getting kind of desperate, I try to get to the Top Man. He's a great guy. I know if I can reach him he'll help a lot. 'Easy does it,' he says, and it sounds easy when he says it."

The Cracker was still recuperating and had been ordered to avoid exertion the day Joe's Doctor precipitated a scene in the ward. The inmate doctor was moving about among the patients making his examinations and conducting interviews. With one convalescant sympathetic to his cause he began a conversation about me. His tongue must have been extremely vitriolic, for it stirred the Cracker to a fury. He rose from his bed, seized a metal chair and brought it down with great violence at the place where the doctor's head had been. Fortunately, the latter had moved hastily and the only damage was to his glasses, which were knocked off and shattered on the floor. Joe's Doctor tarried no longer, but hurried down the corridor and disappeared in the stairway.

The Cracker told me about it afterward. "My knees buckled-like when I stood up—that comes from keeping a man in bed, or I sure would've brained the feller."

"The Lord be praised for buckling knees," I said. "You have time enough to do as it is."

He looked at me soberly. "Yes, there is a mite of truth in that. Sometimes I reckon I can't do what I already got."

Within two months of the beginning of my nursing career my redheaded enemy from H-3 and Clothing Issue appeared in the hospital. I had heard about his reasons for being there both in the dormitory and from the guard assigned to duty in the hospital. (The same man was formerly my shouting boss in Clothing Issue.) Some of Reds' deals had caught up with him, and he had been given a choice of punishments: three days either in the Hole or working at "pots and pans." He had chosen "pots and pans" but this was no picnic and he got himself into the hospital for a hernia operation. On examination he was assured by the chief surgeon that there was no urgency, but he insisted, and after a wrangle in which he was bluntly called a "goldbrick" and a "phoney" he had his way.

Following the operation he came under my care. His attitude toward me had not changed in the least, but he accepted my ministrations as if he were entitled to them and was indignant if I failed in the least detail. Hospitalization did not change Reds' way of life, but simply gave him greater leisure to think up things to want. He wanted to be moved out of the ward into an individual room, and he worked on the idea with his customary insistence and ingenuity. His first plea, directed to Madam Captain, was given in the most ingratiating and pathetic voice, but she brushed him off: "You're a phoney, pure and simple. Every day you've been here you've been cheating pots and pans. You'll stay right where you are."

After she left the room Reds expressed his opinion of her with vitriolic vigor, but that was not the end of his efforts. He bribed some of the nurses with cigarettes and then, supported by them, directed his plea to the second surgeon, who ordered him transferred to a three-patient room—not quite what he wanted, to be sure, but a triumph nevertheless. When Madam Captain stormed, "You're a cheat and a swindler—you bribed my nurses to tell the doctor you should be transferred," he merely smirked.

He wanted clean sheets every day. A patient was entitled to a change twice a week, but he bribed the nurses to give him sheets intended for other patients or to steal extras from the linen locker for his use.

One day while I was tending him he complained that his sheets had not been changed. I told him he would have to wait two days. He protested that he had to have clean sheets, that he always got a change daily.

"Not from me," I told him. "If you must have them get them from Madam or get them for yourself."

To my surprise he accepted the second suggestion. I saw him get out of bed, stand for a moment at the door of his room, then slip cautiously into the corridor. He was on his way to the nurses' office where extra sheets were kept when Madam Captain saw him. She charged down the corridor and drove him back to his cot with a barrage of invectives that might have awed a top sergeant.

Reds also felt the need for special items of food, and he wanted his dinners served in a particular way. He wanted new socks, an elastic belt, and other miscellaneous articles. The persistency and cleverness he displayed in getting the things he wanted was amazing. At uneven intervals Madam Captain would inspect the lockers and confiscate contraband. At times he was caught, and when his prizes were carried off he took satisfaction in telling the world what kind of woman the Captain was—and he had many foul thoughts on the subject.

What an extraordinary fellow he was! The particular things he strove for did not matter much; it was the wanting and the scheming that counted. He had served most of his term by the time he arrived at the hospital, and he managed to stay with us by one complaint or another until he was ready to be paroled; he never did go back to pots and pans. Physically he was rugged, with a zest for living, and I can imagine how busily his mind must have worked the moment he reached the outside world—where there was much to want and scheme for that did matter. I never saw him again, and I often wonder whether he succeeded in playing an errorless game.

13.

FACES IN THE CROWD

The population of my dormitory was always changing. I myself moved away in the latter part of January, but before I left I came to know my roommates well enough, and my status was sufficiently established for me to welcome newcomers. H-3 was still an unhappy place, but the exuberance of its indecency was becoming tamer.

Among the new arrivals was a minister who had been committed for theft in an area under federal jurisdiction, a big-boned man with heavy features and a mass of iron-gray hair. His ministerial character was identifiable in his carriage, his voice, and the form of his speech. The precepts for living to which he declared fealty were beyond reproach in their moral level. His sense of duty was so exacting, for example, that he felt called upon to report all the dishonest doings of the dormitory to the authorities. He was not a "rat" in the customary sense, but the result was the same and he achieved a tragic degree of unpopularity.

I recall, too, rather vividly, a quiet young fellow who was doing ample time on a white-slave charge, reference to which seemed to embarrass him to the point of blushing. He was an administrative clerk and was favored with an end cot just under the translucent window of the washroom through which filtered enough light for him to read by after regular hours. This he frequently did until far past midnight, oblivious to the noise about him. He lived in a world of his own and rarely left it to talk to any of his fellow inmates. He was one of those mentioned by the Top Man as covering up the image that was himself and doing his time in a coma.

I came to know quite well a man called the Rabbi. He was a very learned Jewish fellow. He had been an enemy of mine when I first came to the dormitory, but that had been forgotten and we became friends. He was not an attractive or prepossessing figure and was not popular with the prisoners. His large head was set on a short, shapeless body supported by bowed legs. He walked with his narrow shoulders thrown back as if to counterbalance a bulbous stomach. His hair had receded from his forehead to form an arch from ear to ear which framed his broad face and enhanced the formidable proportions of his nose. All of these features I became used to as I found him an engaging disputant. He knew the world and those who peopled it, and had a keen sense of the comic, not only in others but also in himself.

His life history was intriguing. He was Russian-born and as a mere boy of twelve entered the nihilist movement which broke through the surface so violently in 1905 and was so violently suppressed. With others he escaped to the United States and from this vantage point cheered on the Bolshevik Revolution of 1917. In his mind this represented the fulfilment of the aspirations of his youth, and he continued to be its admiring supporter.

The Rabbi's career in this country was prosaic. He became successful in business, married, and had a son and a daughter. After we became acquainted he talked familiarly of his wife as "Mummy" and of his children for all of whom he had the greatest affection. The stroke that had severed him from them left an ever aching wound. His son was a newspaper man, a feature-writer, and the father had a bundle of clippings which he proudly gave to me to read. They rated a compliment and I gave it, which pleased him.

His trouble with the federal authorities had arisen in the course of his business. He was an insurance broker with a profitable clientele. The Department of Justice had prosecuted him for doing something that, as he told me much aggrieved, was common practice in the insurance business; he felt he had been picked on unfairly as the scapegoat.

In the course of our discussions on many subjects I discovered that he was well acquainted with the Torah and the Talmud and knew almost nothing of the New Testament, so I persuaded him to read portions of it. He did so in a critical spirit, and we had several friendly arguments, neither of us swaying the other's viewpoint, of course.

He had his peculiarities, the most marked of which was an extraordinary ability to concentrate on a single, perhaps trivial goal. At such times he could be obtuse about observing the rights of other people who might be sensitive and quick to take offense. One morning when, as usual, the washbowls were in great demand and we were all lined up waiting our turns, I finally reached one of them. As I stood shaving, standing a step back from the washbowl, I glanced down. There was the Rabbi stooped over at the level of my stomach, splashing his face hastily with water from the bowl.

"Friend Rabbi," I said, "where did you come from?" He twisted his head around and looked up at me in surprise as though he had not been conscious of my presence.

"A thousand pardons," he said, took another splash and ducked out under my arm. He had been watching for an opening, had seen one, and had immediately pounced on it without bothering to notice if he was causing an inconvenience. This trait was exhibited in many ways, and it can be understood why he was not popular in the dormitory.

The hospital's nursing staff had a steady turnover as men went out of jail or were given other assignments; thus it happened that the Rabbi was assigned to the hospital shortly after I was. He appeared one morning a bit before seven o'clock in the nurses' office and with his shoulders and head thrown back announced his name and stated he was reporting for duty. There was a moment's pause as the nurses looked him over; then someone laughed and said, "Oh yeah?" but it did not disturb him. He took up his work and conducted it with a solemnity so out of keeping with his comic figure that he became the butt of considerable jesting the first few times he accompanied a doctor on his rounds. However, he completely ignored it, and soon he had taught himself to be a competent nurse.

There were other personnel changes in our ward—Boots, the janitor, went precipitately, and I felt partly responsible for his departure. I liked the young fellow. He went about his work earnestly and I sensed in him a kind of pathos coupled with an irrepressible sense of humor. When we met in the corridor we saluted each other gravely with a bow and a formal "good morning"; then as we passed he would close his right eye and I would answer wtih the same signal. His large and expressive eyes made his mimicry all the more humorous. But they also caused his undoing.

One day he stood before Madam Captain receiving the usual full and explicit instructions. He accepted them with alert attention; then, as he turned to go, he closed his right eye.

She caught it at once and said sharply, "Put away your mop and report to the administration office. You're dismissed." So we had a new janitor.

The nurses in surgical ward worked in three shifts. One, with a complement of four, began at seven in the morning and went off at three in the afternoon. During this period most of the operations were performed. The next shift extended from three in the afternoon until eleven at night, and the third from eleven until seven the following morning. Sometime in April or May I was assigned to the second shift, which required only two nurses. My partner was the Rabbi, who had suggested this arrangement himself saying that we should constitute a study in international comity. I was satisfied. Our work, except in the case of emergency operations, would be largely routine. We would be pretty much on our own, since Madam Captain departed at three o'clock, and I could anticipate being entertained during slow periods by the Rabbi's continuous flow of perky comment on the world and those who peopled it.

The patients we ministered to changed from day to day. Each afternoon we came in to find some gone and others in their places. Occasionally they were previous acquaintances.

The Baron appeared one day. He had stalked into the hospital, his tall figure bent painfully at the hips by a strain in the sacroiliac region. The chief surgeon had examined him. I managed to reconstruct the interview from what the Baron told me. The Baron's symptoms were subjective. The chief surgeon had been unsympathetic, bluntly expressing his doubts as to their reality. The Baron had undertaken to set him straight in his deliberate Oxfordian English.

"But my good fellow," he had begun, and was cut off.

"I'm not your good fellow; I'm the first surgeon here."

"As you choose. In any event, I assure you I know the cause of my suffering. I have had it before. That time it happened when I was doing something befitting a gentleman. This time I was doing something quite otherwise." He had then proceeded to state the precise nature of the treatment he should receive and the prognosis for his recovery, to all of which the chief surgeon paid little attention, merely muttering something about "smart guy" and "faker."

The Baron concluded his version of the interview with the comment, "Stupid fellow, what? That chief surgeon." He said this not in anger but with a kind of resignation to the fact that the world was peopled with stupid fellows.

The Baron spent his time in the hospital poring over the record of his legal case and his lawyer's brief on appeal. I listened to a number of his remarks to the effect that his lawyer had overlooked vital elements in the case, and I noticed that the brief was scribbled over with a maze of marginal notes and interlineations.

About this time his lawyer visited him, and the pained figure of the Baron made its way from the hospital to the visiting room. The interview became known at once throughout population. It had started sedately enough, but presently the lawyer's voice was heard to rise higher and higher until he was shouting. The lawyer became very red in the neck and finally rose, tossed the papers he held in his hand over the top of the board partition separating him from his client and stalked away without looking back. The Baron brought his rejected manuscript back with him. He told me that he had to put up with a lawyer who was "a regrettably ignorant fellow" and "most stubborn."

Population knew that the Baron had presented many "constructive criticisms" to the prison administration, so many, in fact, that they had become wearisome. They had all added up to a job on the coal pile for him, where his injury had occurred—recurred, as he would have it, the original having been the product of the polo field.

One afternoon I came to work and found the Rabbi bubbling over with a story out of H-3 (I had changed quarters by that time, but he still lived there). He told it with gusto and mimicry. A number of men had been missing prized articles, one a pair of socks, another a pack of cigarettes, still another a pipe, and others pouches of tobacco or lumps of sugar. Each man had been troubled by the loss but had said nothing, thinking himself at fault. Then two of them got together and compared notes, and soon a dozen men were discussing their mutual misfortunes. Finally a revelation struck one big fellow, and he brought a fist down in the palm of his hand and announced, "By god, there's a thief in this jail." They were not long deciding who the thief was. The evidence would not have stood up in court but it was enough for them. They came up behind the suspect in the washroom, threw a blanket over his head, and broke all his fingers.

"You'll find him in the ward," the Rabbi said. "He's the minister you left behind to shepherd our souls when you departed. He's out there on his cot talking like an apostle of your Christ."

I went into the ward and found him. He was suffering considerable pain, with both hands swathed in bandages. When I talked to him, his ministerial character was uppermost, and he expressed himself as resolved to bear his sufferings with Christian fortitude and in the spirit of Christian forgiveness. I had heard of kleptomania as a disease, and now I could see a victim of it.

Paddy, the shoemaker of Clothing Issue, was another victim of kleptomania. Since I left Clothing Issue he had been elevated to the post of runner, being dispatched on errands about the jail. I ran across him once and found him quite chipper about his new assignment. Then one day, everyone in the hospital was called upon to look for the chief's prize pipe, but it couldn't be found. Other things disappeared and the accusing finger was pointed at Paddy. His locker was searched; it was completely innocent, but the missing articles were found in other lockers in the dormitory—lockers of men who could not have done the stealing. So Paddy was convicted and punished and went back to "Clothing Issue." The things he stole were useless to him. They could not be traded and he could not take them with him, but the nimble fingers just had to work.

Dago Blackie appeared in the ward one afternoon, flat on his back on a cot. His tonsils had been removed that morning. He was not a big fellow, but he was strong-muscled and tense. His suffering irritated him and he wanted to fight it. I tried to ease him and told him that if he didn't keep quiet he would merely prolong his trouble. He didn't respond readily to my efforts, but he appreciated them; before he left he was talking rather freely with me about his plans. The administration had gotten wind of his racket of selling protection and had broken up his gang, but he had a new idea which he was going to put into effect as soon as he got going again.

Another of my patients was a young fellow who had raped and murdered his mother's closest friend. He had been brought directly to the hospital upon his admission to jail and, when I saw him, was a mere rack of bones, so neurotic that it was difficult to tell whether or not he was sane. He was really a mental case who should have been placed in the second-floor psych ward, but there were no private rooms available there and we had one empty. He remained, however, under the jurisdiction of the psychiatrist and psychologist who examined and cross-examined him and decided he was a homosexual. What relation that had to his crime I don't know.

He was under my care for one-third of the day, and for some reason he seemed to take comfort out of talking to me, and he clung to me eagerly. I found that he was haunted by what he had done and was groping out for somebody to whom he might tell the story. When he began telling it an intent stare came into his eyes as if the scene reappeared before him. He wanted to develop all the details—how he had killed his victim, how he had disposed of each particular part of the body. It was a gruesome story. If he had been confessing preparatory to expiating his crime I might have listened, but I soon discovered he wasn't. He was simply reliving it and feeling again the ecstasy that came with his act. It was too strong a dose for my constitution. I never heard the end of the story. Before long he was sent to a federal institution where incurable cases are confined.

Then there was a banker from the Middle West, a man well beyond sixty who had undergone a gland operation; infection had set in, and it threatened to be serious. He was quite convinced he was going to die. I can remember him as he lay on his cot, very still. His head on the pillow showed a strong profile and struck me as being a good model for some sort of commemorative bankers' medallion. I became his intimate in the quick, natural way one does under such circumstances, and I soon learned that he had been a man of importance in his part of the country, the owner of ranches and farms as well as a banker. I set the pictures of his wife and his tall sons and daughters opposite his bed where he could see them, and when he was feeling especially bad he asked me to pray for him. I told him that I had done so many times in my mind, but he wanted it out loud. Our chaplain was a Baptist, the patient an Episcopalian; the forms of his church are closely related to the Lutheran, and he longed for the familiar words.

The request was embarrassing, for I could not invade the province of the chaplain without special permission from the warden, and this called for intricate negotiations. However, permission was secured. Then it fell upon me to conjure up the right things to say, no easy matter at such a time. I tried to make my prayer sincere and sympathetic, drawing largely from Bible passages which we all know, the grandeur and beauty of which exalt us and make mundane things—even death itself—seem of small importance. I hope I comforted him. In any event he survived the night and ultimately recovered.

A colored minister, very black and monstrously stout, became one of our charges. I had heard of him in population. Sometimes he would feel called upon to exhort his dormitory as if it were a congregation. His voice would start at a low pitch, rising higher and higher until its great booming tones filled the place and drew a chorus of "amens" from his spellbound listeners. He had been brought to the hospital for a hemorrhoid operation. The operation itself is not serious, but the recovery is troublesome—packing is required, and by the third day the patient is in a bad way indeed. Three days after the minister's operation I came upon him writhing and tossing and clutching at his bedclothes. His emotions were high, and he was carrying on a conversation with himself in which he charged the first surgeon, who had done the operation, with all sorts of evil intentions. The surgeon was a Missourian, and the minister claimed he had "no use for niggers." As I approached he turned to me and said in his deep voice, "The damn surgeon sewed me up. I know it and I'm going to die; that's why he did it."

He was working himself into something of a frenzy. I tried to quiet him, but he prayed loudly for me to save him. I knew it was time for the packing to be removed, so I got him to lie still while I injected a dose of mineral oil and permitted it to soak in; then, with a quick twist, I drew out the packing. He gave an agonized scream at the sudden sharp pain, but relief followed; and thereafter he placed more reliance upon me than upon all the doctors.

It fell to the lot of the Rabbi to care for the minister the following day, and when his work was completed and we were together in the office he gave me a detailed account of his feelings in a voice of utter solemnity. He drew a picture of himself approaching the vast black twin-mountains, he reviewed the thoughts that flitted through his mind as he hung precariously over the crater, and he told of his ultimate thanksgiving when he withdrew in safety.

At the end of several months the Rabbi himself fell ill. We kept him in the surgical ward and I carried on alone. Whenever I had an opportunity I talked to him. He was a very sick man, but through it all occasional sparks of humor flickered in his speech. But at times, when he was alone with his thoughts, the tears would trickle down his face, their course divided by the great ridge of his nose, and I could hear him murmuring, "Mummy. . . . Oh! Mummy." He was ill for many weeks but eventually rejoined me on the second shift.

In letters to my wife I usually said little about life in jail and never named persons, but I notice that one, dated in the latter part of July, has the following passages:

> In the morning I play—if the weather permits—shuffleboard with my colleague from the hospital. He is Jewish Orthodox and well versed in Hebrew so I have a chance to refresh my Hebrew studies. Once in a while we even get a good laugh during the game.

Of my work in the surgical ward I wrote:

> My faith there is satisfied with God's choice for my life. As great as my longing is to serve in His Name in His Church, wherever I can spread his Holy Word, yet I see His ways even here in prison, and I try to serve Him with humble mind and heart, even if it is only a cooling drink of water that I can give to a sick inmate here in the prison hospital, or make a bed for a helpless one, or—forgive me that I mention it—help him to a bedpan. What does it matter what kind of service I render as long as I follow our Master and do His will? Let me learn from Him day by day, "All things work together for good to them that love God."

14.

APPEALS AND DECISIONS

It was nearly five months after I became a convict before my appeal to the Circuit Court of Appeals in New York City began to take tangible form. In the middle of January, 1943, I was permitted to receive a copy of the printed brief prepared by my lawyers. I read it carefully and began to comprehend the real gist of my case and the basis upon which my conviction stood. It seemed impossible for a man to be convicted on such a basis, and my confidence in the success of the appeal was strengthened. I began to lean upon it more than I realized.

A friend had subscribed to the *New York Times* in my behalf, and I received it daily. In the issue of February 12 I read that my case had been argued before the court a day earlier and had been taken under advisement. There was nothing for me to do but wait for the answer. What would it be? It carried inexpressible meaning for me.

My wife's faith was steadfast. She believed it was the will of God that justice should ultimately prevail. My lawyers, one in Philadelphia, the other in Hartford, Connecticut, wrote frequently. At first they had been lawyers in an unpopular cause, but now they were loyal friends and devoted adherents. In their letters they wrote that their faith in me and my cause had never faltered and that they had hopes that the appellate court would reverse my conviction. There was nothing I could do but pray and prepare myself to accept as God's will whatever the result might be. Toward the end of March I wrote, "Six weeks have passed by since the hearing of the appeal. . . . The time of waiting is a great test of patience and faith."

My lawyer from Philadelphia visited me on April 1; he cheered me by his hopes. My wife visited me the following day; she was calmly confident. I was lifted by them to a state of assurance I had never felt before. The caution I had built up against too great reliance upon the Court of Appeals weakened, and I suddenly found my spirits leaping forward to the moment when I should be vindicated and this nightmare I was living should be ended by a judicial decree declaring the whole thing a mistake, a sort of hideous perversion of a joke. The dream was demoralizing. I had to smother it. I had to be prepared for anything. I remembered what had happened at Hartford. It could not have happened, but it did.

It was the morning of Saturday, the third day of April. I was in the nurses' office when the Swede came in and expressed his sympathy. The other nurses frowned at him, but it was too late; he had heard of my appeal being dismissed on the loudspeaker that morning, and came to offer his condolences. This was how I got the news. I learned later that the other nurses had agreed to tell me nothing of it, but the Swede had not been there when the agreement was made. He assumed that I knew and came at once to see me, thinking I would be in need of friendly sympathy and encouragement. He meant well, of course, but he delivered a hard blow. I wrote to my wife:

> When I received the sad news—so unbelievable—for a moment I felt suddenly defenseless, forsaken and alone in an unfriendly world. . . . I know how you and the children must feel. . . . But do not lose faith, hope, and courage. When I came back to my cell after I had heard the sad news I got my Bible—looking and longing for a guiding word. And this I found, when I opened the New Testament.

148

Hebrews 13:5-6: "He hath said, I will never leave thee or forsake thee. So that we may boldly say, The Lord is my helper, and I will not fear what man shall do unto me."

My elderly lawyer friend in Philadelphia wrote to me, "My heart goes out to you in your great trouble." I thought of him with affection and could picture his thin esthetic face and finely modeled profile, his fringe of white hair and his gray mustache. But more clearly still I could remember his spirit, somewhat wistful and detached. It showed in the expression of his eyes and made you feel his concern with matters that others passed by. His detachment enhanced, perhaps, by his difficulty in hearing, but, as others told me, he was always that way—always looking for a cause calling for martyrdom, a cause no one else would advocate and within which lay kernels of injustice troubling to him and to him alone.

He was widely known in the city of his birth where his family has had its roots for several centuries. He was a friend of President Woodrow Wilson, under whom he served as United States Attorney for Eastern Pennsylvania. His tenure of office extended through the first world war, when he came under criticism for not being sufficiently ruthless. He told me once in his contemplative way that, looking back, it was quite clear that ruthlessness had not been at all necessary. In 1920 he resigned his office in protest against the Red Raids.

On several occasions during the course of my trial we traveled to Hartford together on the train and discussed many things. I found him a student of the Bible, many passages of which he could recite by heart. One in particular I recall, for he asked me for my interpretation of it. It is the following verse from Psalm 85:

> Mercy and truth are met together; righteousness and peace have kissed each other. Truth shall spring out of the earth; and righteousness shall look down from heaven. Yea, the Lord shall give that which is good.

There was an emotional beauty in the lines that haunted his memory and an elusiveness of meaning that intrigued him. Neither of us could recall either Greek or Hebrew texts, and we speculated upon the exact words that had been translated into the King James Version. Of one thing I am sure—I shall always think of him when I read Psalm 85.

He and many others were in my mind as I wrote to my wife that it comforted me when "my heart and thoughts turn to you and the children and our many, many friends and to all those who are so wonderful and faithful to us." My lawyer in Connecticut was also among these; he had become a friend whose faith never faltered. He had taken us into his home during the month-long trial.

At times of great emotional shock a man is fortunate to have daily duties which require performing service to others. I had duties demanding my best efforts in the hospital, and I also had duties to my children. My younger daughter and my son were to be confirmed in the church in May, and my wife asked me to provide the appropriate Bible verses to give them as a blessing. "The silenced voice of a silent pastor may be louder than ever," my wife wrote. For my son I chose Hebrews 13:5-6, the passage quoted above. For my younger daughter, the baby, I chose Matthew 5:8, "Blessed are the pure in heart: for they shall see God."

My children had never visited me in jail. At the time of the trial in Hartford we had sent them away to stay with friends outside Philadelphia. Now both my wife and I were worried about what effect a visit to me in jail might have upon them, but we finally decided that they should face it; shortly before the date set for their confirmation, they visited me. I wrote of the occasion in my next letter:

It was indeed a highlight. How our children are growing! . . . It was some sort of a confirmation service for the children and for all of us. At least I could bless my children with the words of the Bible which I selected for them for this sacred occasion, and I could do it personally. They are confirmed by their father anyhow—may God bless them and lead them on the right road of life so that they may in the midst of all the darkness of this world walk as children of light.

I was nevertheless troubled, and expressed my concern over the impact of this meeting on the children in letters to my wife. They were old enough to understand what had happened to me, and I had been at a loss to read their thoughts at our meeting. My son in particular seemed very quiet. I hoped that what had happened to me would not make them hard and bitter.

The petition to the Supreme Court was duly filed. On June 14, 1953, it was denied, and in my letter of June 16 I wrote:

> I cannot write very much, just to let you know that my heart goes out for you and the children. . . . Yesterday I read in the Philadelphia *Inquirer* that my petition had been denied. My lawyer and friend from Philadelphia came the same day to strengthen me. Words fail me to say what and how I feel. . . . No one can tell what will come of it all. All the things we took for granted as stable and unchanging —all the ideals of freedom, right and justice—are rocking under our feet, but in all the uncertainty I feel absolutely certain that we shall be together again. I know that we are together in our deepest feelings and thoughts. The clouds of our deep sense of gloom and tragic futility will someday clear up again and will make mankind feel ashamed of having lacked the power . . . to break the bonds which tie him to unrighteousness. Sometimes I wish to become angry. I cannot. I place everything in the Eternal's hands. He will see to it that justice will be done.

The decision of the Supreme Court made another decision necessary. I was still pastor of Old Zion. My congregation had stood by me faithfully, but now that the last chance in the courts had been snuffed out, the church had to get a new pastor. In a letter to the congregation I told them this, but I declined to demit the ministry in spite of a few panicked individuals who wished me to do so. I had done nothing to warrant demission.

Under the impact of a psychological blow our spirits sometimes respond by becoming exalted. Later they may subside, as mine did now, into a sodden mass. I found it more and more difficult to control my anger. From my cell window I could look over the west wall of the jail. In June the country round about was ripening with a fruitful beauty; I meditated on its peaceful serenity and thought, "It is only man that is hateful." But I fought off my bitterness and gave myself more earnestly than ever to my work in prison.

As long as my appeal had been pending I must have felt subconsciously that my situation was a temporary horror which would someday end abruptly. Then I would emerge into the sunlight, be reunited with my family and friends, and pick up the severed strands of my life. Now the outside world seemed to recede to a great distance. It was still there, and I could still see the faces and hear the voices of those I knew, but they were fading objects belonging to another dimension —one to which I felt I could never belong. I was alive but entombed, and my return at some remote time in the future would be like that of a man coming back from the dead.

Ahead of me stretched endlessly the daily repetition of prison routine. On September 3, 1943, the 375th day of my imprisonment, I wrote to my wife that "prison days are like tears filtering down slow and heavy."

15.

THE DRUG ROOM

In mid-August of 1943 I could write that some change had taken place in my work, that I was now clerk in the drug room of the hospital. In my letter this appears as a casual remark, for I never went into detail in referring to life in the jail. But it was a change of great significance, both to me and to many others. It had come about in this way.

The man called "Irish" was "getting short"—that is, nearing the time for his release. Officially known as the prison pharmacist, to population he was known as the man in charge of the drug room, located on the first floor of the hospital. At times I had gone to visit him there. At other times I had met him when he visited the surgical ward, so I had come to know him and part of his story. He had put in nearly thirteen years of his twenty-year sentence, almost enough for the conditional release promised him after completion of two-thirds of the sentence. He talked freely about it and could tell you the date and the day of the week he was due to go out. His original sentence had been eighty years. It had been reduced to forty, then to twenty, and now as a man approaching middle age he was looking forward to an adventure so dazzling that it almost blinded him.

He had been a sergeant in the regular army in the days on the other side of that thirteen-year chasm, and though the story of his trouble had faded into colorlessness the version that persisted told of the time he was custodian of a stable

153

of cavalry horses and of his joining forces with a bottle during the performance of his duty. There was a fire and a holocaust of horses, and the court martial found him guilty of arson. He had started doing his time in the penitentiary at Atlanta and had been transferred to Lewisburg when the new jail was completed. He had been the official pharmacist in our prison for many years—hence he was a personage of some importance. He acted the part. He felt responsible towards only two superiors, the Chief and the warden. To them he gave quick military attention and the deference due their rank. Madam Captain he had known in Atlanta, and still battled with her on familiar terms.

To the doctors, particularly the newer members of the staff, Irish could be emphatically curt—often with justification—when they presumed upon their rank to get items of the precious drug-room stock outside of properly authorized channels. One such battle was staged when I was there. The doctor was the psychiatrist, a branch of the profession which aroused no respect at all in Irish. He asked for a certain drug and Irish refused to surrender it. The doctor then rephrased his request as an order issued by both an officer of the Public Health Service and a member of the medical profession. The issue was joined. Irish's weapons were blunt and forthright. He ended his attack by saying, "Sure, you're a doctor, and sure enough I'm a pharmacist, but I'm a quack pharmacist and you're a quack doctor. Get the Chief's signature on your order and I'll fill it."

Out in population Irish, as custodian and dispenser of much-desired items, was the center of much attention. It was maintained that with know-how and the proper connections, you could gain certain highly regarded favors from Irish. Thus, as the time for his release drew nearer, gossip about his possible successor became more and more intense—for some it was a matter of grave concern. Among the names mentioned as probable "heirs" were those of two men in the X-ray room—among the hospital nurses these were top favorites in the running because they were "naturals" and had influential backing. In the stockade other names were discussed, including those of several pharmacist-inmates. The Top Man was approached for his opinion; he was expected to know about such things and to know also how to influence the course of events. He would listen in his attentive way and reply in his deep mellow voice, seemingly able to gratify his questioners without committing himself.

But once he told me privately that he was not mixing in the pharmacy affair at all. "I watch my step. I do make a good many suggestions to the warden, and frequently he wants them, for they're helpful to him and to the rest of us. But I won't tell the men that the pharmacy is out of my field, and so, when the selection is made, likely as not I'll get credit for it."

I was in the nurses' office one afternoon when Irish came through the doorway, marched to the middle of the room and halted. "How are you, Reverend?" he barked. Then he paused as if trying to think of a strategic opening, abandoned the idea, and announced bluntly, "I'm getting short, you know. I've got just over four months to go. I've talked to the Chief about my successor, and he agrees with me that you are the man."

I looked at him with surprise. "I don't understand that. I have no training for such work."

He answered, "That's all right—you have education, and the job isn't so tough when you get to know it. I'll be around for a while yet and can break you in."

There was little more he could think of to say, and he departed as abruptly as he had come. I had no further notice of my assignment, so the next afternoon I reported to the third floor. It was shortly before three o'clock, and Madam Captain was preparing to go. She stopped me as I entered.

"What are you doing here? You're reporting to pharmacy."

"I have no orders," I replied. "Irish spoke to me about it yesterday, but I was doubtful of his authority."

She sniffed. "Irish was right. It's the only time I can remember him being right. You can report to the Chief for orders."

The Chief's office was on the first floor. In an anteroom sat his new stenographer, a young woman from the world beyond the walls who excited a deal of curiosity on the part of the prisoners. Her predecessor had married an inmate upon his release; how they managed their courting is their affair. The young woman was expecting me and directed me to the Chief's office.

I found him seated behind a flat-topped desk smoking a pipe. I sat facing him, and he said, "Reverend, the warden and I have agreed that you should take charge of the pharmacy. You can begin at once in order to get accustomed to the duties before Irish leaves."

"Irish spoke to me about it yesterday," I replied, "but I doubted his authority. It seemed too extraordinary. My knowledge of drugs and chemicals is almost nil, and I thought since there were pharmacist inmates. . . ."

He smiled and cut me off. "We've considered them and passed them by. This is a position, as you perhaps know, of considerable responsibility. We want someone we can trust."

It was my turn to smile. "I wonder what Washington would think of that. It treats me as a highly suspicious character and listens in to every word I say to visitors and reads everything I write—which must be quite a bore to somebody."

He ignored my comment and went on: "I spent several

years in Germany at the Stuttgart consulate. I know something of the training given in chemistry in the German schools. I think you can master the job, and we have confidence in our choice."

"Well," I said, "I shall try to justify your confidence, but I wish I could share it."

He replied, "I assure you that I'll do my best to help you, and so will the other members of the staff." Then as I was going he said, "I think you'll find it a good place to do time. I gather that among the inmates the big hand of the clock seems to move at the gait of the small one. It won't always be that way in pharmacy."

Going from the doctor's office to the drug room I passed the hospital administration office, which was separated from the hallway by a waist-high counter. In this office were the administrative officers of the Public Health Service and several inmate clerks. My relations with these officials had never been cordial, but one of them came up to the counter as I passed by and assured me that he was much pleased with my selection and was sure we could work together. I thanked him, but I was not much impressed. He was not rated highly among the inmates, and the Top Man had already warned me against lending him money, adding, "I've marked my loans to him off the books." The warning had been quite unnecessary, for I had the best defense in the world against unwise loans. I had no money to lend.

The entrance to the drug room was through a door split like a Dutch door; the lower half, with a shelf attached, could be left closed while the upper half was open. When I entered Irish greeted me in his heavy fashion, while his colored helper, who was Boots, the former janitor of the surgical ward, welcomed me with a cheerful grin and a wink of his right eye.

The room was lighted by three large windows on the north

157

wall opposite the entrance. Spanning the space beneath them was a waist-high slate shelf holding laboratory equipment—scales and flasks and a Bunsen burner. Above the shelf were racks of test tubes and flasks. To the left, where the north wall met the west wall, was a sink with spigots and a disorderly array of empty bottles and flasks on the shelf beside it. In the space beyond the window to the right was a medicine cabinet. There were more medicine cabinets and steel lockers against the other three walls.

After a few moments of preliminary conversation Irish cleared his throat and began his lecture. He flung open the door of the first steel locker on the left. It stood higher than my head and its shelves were crowded with stainless steel and glass containers, each with a label. He recited the names on the labels and added incidental comments:

"Here's our sugar in hundred-pound cans—it's for medical purposes, but sugar isn't easy to get. Everybody wants it and you'll have to watch it. This is magnesium sulphate in the stainless steel containers—we make milk of magnesia out of it mixed with a touch of peppermint oil. When the time comes to prepare it I'll show you how it's done; we need a lot of it. In these glass jars, brown and blue, is mineral oil—liquor petrolatum, they call it on the label, but it's just oil to me. We use it for a lot of things, elixirs and the like.

"In these containers is Vaseline, twenty-five pounds of it in the little ones and fifty pounds in the big ones. Some of it's white and some yellow. We use that for ointments and salves and mix it with a lot of things—tannic acid, carbolic acid, menthol, mercury, tar, turpentine, and the like. Most of them are kept in this and the next locker. You'll get to know them so you can find them in the dark. Potassium sulphate is in these cans. It looks kind of brownish and hard, as you see it here, but you usually dissolve it in water. In these fifty-pound cans is powdered boric acid. You make eyewash out of that, dissolved in eighteen parts of water. Here's zinc oxide, also a powder. In these cans is bicarbonate of soda; we use a lot of that.

"Look hard at these gallon bottles of ethyl alcohol—they'll always be on your conscience. Guard them like your right eye; the stuff just naturally leaks out on you. There's a barrel of it in the storeroom down in the basement, next to the morgue. We must have seventy or eighty thousand dollars' worth of drugs and chemicals stored down there. Some of them, like quinine, bring big prices on the outside. You go there on Mondays and Wednesdays to get your supplies for the drug room, and the guard always goes with you. He's not allowed to enter the storeroom; he just stands at the door and watches you. A man from the administration office goes along to watch the guard, and still the stuff disappears. There ought to be another man to watch the man who watches the guard. Beside each shelf in that room is an inventory card. When you take something out you have to mark it out. In the corner you'll see that barrel of alcohol. It looks tight, but sometimes the stuff disappears as if it were leaking at every seam. We just built a special compartment for it with a steel-barred door opened by a special key. That caulked its seams—no leaks so far. We use a lot of alcohol making cough syrup; I'll show you how we do it. It's popular stuff and if we gave out all that was asked for we'd need an extra detail of mixers."

He paused for breath and then continued rolling out cabalistic names and comment. "Here's the telephone connecting you with the captain's desk. You're going to have calls telling you to get something in a hurry." At the sink in the corner, surrounded by quantities of bottles, flasks, and test tubes, he stopped. "This is Boots's part of the establishment. Hey Boots, how about it? Have you got many bottles to wash?"

"Sure have," said Boots. "When I get out of this place I never want to see no more bottles. I see them in my dreams, an army of them, all dirty and all waitin' to be washed."

Beyond the sink on the waist-high slate shelf next to it was a distilling apparatus. Irish grew eloquent: "We use this for distilling water and when she gets to hissing and burbling she gets plenty of notice from population. All the guys who knew something about stills on the outside come to attention—mostly they're from the South. They stop at the door and lean in over the shelf and say, 'What's cookin', buddy,' and I say, 'Water, that's all, nothin' but water.' Mostly they don't believe me. They look at the contraption as if they'd like to play with it."

We moved along the slate shelf. Irish pointed to the racks of test tubes and flasks and the weighing scales. "Here's where you mix your stuff: milk of magnesia—you make four gallons of it at a time every two weeks; the horehound cough syrup; the lotions and ointments; the elixirs; and Dobell's solution for a gargle. That Dobell's solution is somethin'. To make it you start with bicarbonate of soda dissolved in lukewarm distilled water, then you pour in glycerine and mix with phenol—pure carbolic—and that raises a hell of a fuss. You have to go easy or it'll boil up all over you. That concoction is a son-of-a-bitch. You got something there that could blow the lid off this joint."

He pointed to the medicine cabinet beyond the last window. "This," he said, "is always locked. There are poisons in there: potassium cyanide and bichloride of mercury, used as antiseptics; procaine hydrochloride, used as an anesthetic; sodium salicylate; aspirin, and a lot of other things." We turned to the east wall, in the middle of which was another medicine cabinet. "It's not so necessary to keep this one locked," he remarked. "This contains bottled stuff all made up and ready for general use. You can't let it out, though, except on a doctor's prescription, and the label on the bottle has to be signed by the pharmacist. Otherwise it's contraband and it's confiscated wherever it's found." At the corner where the east wall met the front wall, there were wooden stands filled with crutches and canes. "You give these out only on doctor's orders, and you take a receipt for them. You notify the captain's desk of the issue, then you keep close check with the doctors and get them back as soon as they're not needed any more. They're dangerous weapons out in population. You can get a hell of a wallop from a crutch."

Against the front wall was a little locker about three feet high. He pointed to this and said, "Here's another one we always keep locked. Here's where we put the overflow of dangerous stuff, the kind we have in the first cabinet I showed you. But these two big cabinets next to it aren't always kept locked. They hold ointments and salves that have been made up and are ready for use—only on a doctor's prescription, of course."

Last came the refrigerator: "That is always under lock and key. There's dope inside: morphine, codeine, Veronal, phenobarbital, Luminal, Amytal. There are needles made up for injections of the stuff, and penicillin and insulin needles too. You have to guard that refrigerator like your right eye. The dope peddlers and dope addicts know it's there, and somehow a bit of it gets out."

We had completed our round; I was properly bewildered and overwhelmed by the immense knowledge of my companion. Later when I catalogued all the chemicals and drugs and derivatives they tallied more than twelve hundred, each with its individual properties. But now I sensed them only as a jungle which I could never penetrate.

We were standing contemplating the problem, I with my

161

back to the door, when I heard someone walking along the corridor. Whoever it was spoke to Irish, who nodded stiffly in return, and then the footsteps passed on. Irish looked at me. "Joe's Doctor," he said, "a son-of-a-bitch. Don't trust him. He gets stuff out of here somehow. I sure would like to catch him at it. And he don't like you. Don't trust those guys next door, either." He jerked his thumb toward the administration office. "One of those guys—I guess I don't have to tell you which one—is a gambler, and he always needs money. He has his quarters over the administration building, and the wall keeps his creditors out just like it keeps us in. Some of this stuff here brings a high price on the outside—these vitamin tablets, for one thing. This guy is the one who watches the guard who watches you when you go to the storeroom. Never let him inside.

"Some of these staff doctors, too, act as if they were entitled to get what they wanted. Don't let 'em bluff you. Make them write a prescription. This is all government stuff. Everybody thinks it belongs to the world, but if it gets away from you it's your hard luck."

Irish's first lecture to me had been in part a pretentious display of knowledge and in part hardheaded, solid advice. It was to be only the beginning of my education.

Every morning at eleven o'clock the line formed for sick call, filling the passageway that led into the hospital between the X-ray room on one side and the medical library on the other. On busy days the tail of the line was out in the main corridor of the jail. A guard sat at the inner end and let the prisoners pass one at a time. The Chief sat in the corridor by the counter of the administration office, a clerk at his side holding the files of all the visiting patients. As each man came up, his file was picked out and presented to the Chief, who then had a medical history before him on which to base his interview. The interviews were brief, but they were gratifying moments for the prisoners. The doctor took a personal interest in the man, who became for an instant a person instead of a number. A prescription would be made out on a master card, then passed to the clerk behind the counter who brought it to a window in the wall separating the administration office from the drug room. We took it and prepared the prescription for delivery at our door. If it took a while the patient would sit on a bench outside of the drug room and wait until we finished.

The prescriptions were mostly harmless: Epsom salts, cough syrup, milk of magnesia, salves and ointments, or tablets of many varieties, all duly labeled and signed by the pharmacist. It was curious to note how familiar the names of many things became to me after a week or more as Irish's assistant.

At certain hours the diabetics came for their injections, which were given by the doctor whose office was across the corridor from the drug room. Among these I recognized the elderly movie magnate I had met in H-3. Wednesday was the day for the venereal-disease patients, nearly two hundred of them—about 10 per cent of population—some of whom were embarrassed and full of voluble explanations about the source of their trouble. We had to prepare their injections and give them to the doctor across the way.

At intermittent times throughout the day men would come on passes for special medical attention. Sometimes their cases called for prescriptions; sometimes they passed by us on the way to the ear, nose, and throat clinic or the dental clinic or the room set aside for electrotherapy and hydrotherapy treatments. Accident cases, of which there were a great variety, went to the emergency clinic.

Pharmacy did a heavy business on a busy street, and I became acquainted with most of population.

163

16.

FROM 'REVEREND' TO 'DOC'

Irish showed me the ordinary processes and techniques of the pharmacy. I watched him perform, and his dexterity and confidence were amazing to me; but his interest in teaching soon faded and within a month or two I was called upon to rely almost entirely on myself. The thought of his rapidly approaching day of delivery kept Irish in a state of continual excitement, called by some the "jitters." He would come to the drug room in the morning as if he intended to settle down to doing his accustomed work, but in no time he would be off visiting the wards. The only place he could stay for any length of time was the Chief's outer office, where he might be seen sitting, without a word, just watching the young woman secretary. His behavior puzzled me until I heard some jocular fellow explain: "I told Irish there were creatures like that everywhere in the outside world. He hasn't seen one for thirteen years except in the moving pictures, and he's exposing himself like you would to sunburn to build up immunity."

But pharmacy had to go on, and it fell to me to make it do so. I had to learn fast; even so, it was the better part of a year before I felt reasonably confident of my capability. One of the simpler jobs was the preparation of milk of magnesia, which was in constant demand. It consists of magnesium sulphate suspended in distilled water, with a touch of peppermint oil added. The trick lay in securing the suspension, which was accomplished by stirring carefully for twenty-four hours. I learned to mix ointments, salves, and lotions of varied composition, and as time went on and I acquired greater confidence I added some of my own mixtures to the variety. I also had to learn how to mix solutions for sterilizing surgical instruments. Our little still was constantly busy, for its product was used in countless preparations.

Penicillin at that time had just become widely known. It was in short supply in the outside world, but we had it in little bottles hermetically sealed with rubber stoppers. The contents were only a thin precipitate of brownish or yellow dust on the sides and bottom. It was dissolved in sterile, distilled water injected through the rubber stopper with a hypodermic syringe, resulting in a solution containing one hundred thousand units of penicillin. The rubber stopper sealed itself as the needle was withdrawn. Then the solution could be drawn off in hypodermic needles, usually to fill a prescription for immediate use. When it was not used at once, we placed the filled needles in the refrigerator, where the temperature was several degrees above freezing, to prevent the solution from losing its potency.

The small white crystals of procaine hydrochloride were also dissolved in distilled, sterile water, then preserved in hermetically sealed one-ounce bottles; it was used for spinal injections to produce local anesthesia. The strength of the solution depended on the expected length of the operation. A similar solution of chloral hydrate, a sweet-smelling substance, could produce anesthesia when taken by mouth. It had to be carefully guarded, for an overdose would produce sleep that might be eternal.

Mixing Dobell's solution was as interesting as Irish had said it would be. We started with bicarbonate of soda dissolved in a gallon of distilled water; then came 755 cc's of glycerine, to which was added 30 cc's of carbolic acid, which did not improve the temper of the concoction. It had to be poured cautiously. When the stuff had calmed down, three more gallons of distilled water were added, making it fit to be bottled for distribution.

The formula that intrigued me most was the one for horehound cough syrup. First we took horehound tea leaves from the bag where our supply was kept; it had come from the dried and dusty bales in the storeroom. I leaned over the slate shelf carefully weighing out four ounces of tea leaves on my chemist's scales, feeling somewhat like an old-fashioned necromancer preparing to brew his mysterious compounds, and through my mind would run the formula for the famous concoction prepared by the three witches on a Scottish heath. The leaves were placed in a stainless steel gallon container, constructed by prison industries, which was filled with distilled water, then placed on a hot plate next to Boots's bottling department. After being kept at a slow boil for half an hour, it was allowed to cool; then it was strained through a paper filter and the leaves were wrung dry through a linen cloth. This tea was then augmented by simple syrup, ethyl alcohol, and smaller quantities of quill, ipecac, and brown calomel. The mixture was stirred and then poured into small bottles ready for distribution. With its 16 per cent alcohol content and its touch of chloroform, its popularity with the inmates was unmistakable.

I had learned these and many other tasks in a relatively short time. The Chief, as good as his word, aided me considerably, as did his staff and Boots, who was always at hand and was a cheerful helper. I think he spoke well of me out in population among the other Negroes, for they treated me as if they counted me a friend.

The Chief had provided me with a small but weighty library,

which I kept on my desk. It included the National Formulae for United States Pharmacists; the Pharmacopoea, the Pharmaceutical Dictionary and Medical Dictionary. He also got me a subscription to a monthly magazine, *The Pharmacist,* which carried current news of the profession, and many were the times he came in to see me and give the answers to my questions. On occasion the staff physicians would be asked to meet in the pharmacy to discuss its problems; among others, Joe's Doctor attended. He had ceased denouncing me and was polite to me, but I suspect he still did not like me, and I did not trust him.

It was strange how the jungle of bottles and labels was becoming less tangled—one item after another began to stand out as an acquaintance, and the whole bewildering array began to take on an orderly appearance. With the aid of my "library" I could read of the characteristics of my charges. I began to feel familiar with their personalities and to learn how they might be made to co-operate with others. My mind began to be peopled with them, and I could write reverently of "God's thoughts in therapy." The development of understanding gratified me, and I discovered that at times when I had rush orders to fill the big hand on the clock actually seemed to move too fast. The Chief was right. Pharmacy was a good place to do time.

In October, 1943, I was called for my second annual interview with the prison board. This time I knew every member and each knew me. The interview would have been a mere formality if the associate warden had not suggested that I act as an assistant to the Protestant chaplain in conducting church services. He explained that some of the inmates seemed to look to me for spiritual and religious advice. He felt they might take more readily to preaching from a fellow inmate than from an outsider.

I thought the proposal over before I replied. Then I spoke. "Gentlemen, I consider the suggestion complimentary, and I appreciate it as such. It is true that some do come to me for comfort, and I listen to their stories, which is the greatest of all comforts. I may even give advice—and for those who adhere to the Christian faith I can give it in the words and with the allusions to which they respond—but I give advice only to those who seek it. No, I am sure I could not stand up before them and preach. It would not ease their hurt or mine. I have to serve most of them in pharmacy, and the way I serve them there can be the best sermon I could deliver."

Near the end of 1943 I came into sole command of the drug room. Irish had gone out of the great gate with the official $10 in his pocket and the final admonitions of the warden in his mind. It was the day he had waited for. Some of those who knew him were apprehensive and expressed their worries:

"It's going to be tough sledding for Irish. He's been penned up nearly fourteen years living by prison rules. That makes something happen to you."

"He's going out into a world where nobody gives a damn about him. Nobody cares whether he eats or starves; nobody deals out a hospital pass if he's sick; nobody cares whether he gets up in the morning or goes to bed at night; nobody makes sure he's got a roof over his head or a bed to lie on."

"He's not a crook, so he has no profession to slip back into. He spoke of his parents somewhere out along the Pacific coast."

"Thirteen years make a change in parents as well as in sons."

"Irish feels some of that. He went out to the car, head up, strutting like a top sergeant, but inside he was just plain scared."

I had the last news of him from our hospital guard, who had seen him on the station platform at Lewisburg: "I pretended not to know him. He was putting on a front that was supposed to be perfectly natural, but he was as self-conscious as if he had placards back and front with tall letters saying, 'I am a convict just out of the Lewisburg Pen.' I saw him take the train. He was headed for the West Coast. Those placards won't drop off him for a long time yet, and it'll be longer still before his mind gets out of the prison groove—if it ever does. I hope he makes it. He was a crusty guy, but all right at bottom."

After my predecessor's departure I found myself spending more and more time in the pharmacy. At night it was quiet, and I could sit at my desk and write letters, read, or study. Frequently I stayed as late as nine o'clock, the hour for retiring. This was a convenience for the staff physicians. When they were off duty and an emergency call came through, they could refer the matter to me, if it was not too serious.

In stockade I was now a prominent man, and many inmates sought my advice as if I were a doctor; in fact, my old title of "Reverend" began to fade into "Doctor" or "Doc." Attention was often drawn to me when the loudspeaker, used to issue commands and make announcements, would blare out, "Number 12150 wanted in the hospital at once." Quite without my asking I had achieved a significant postion in the social structure of population.

Not long after Irish left I became aware of the fact that some of my drugs were being taken. I marked a faint circle about the base of the bottles I thought had been tapped, and in that way I made certain that somebody was moving them. Who it was I did not know. I discussed the matter with the Chief. The keys to the pharmacy and the locked cabinets were hung on a board in his office when not in use, since it was necessary to have them always available. He deliberated for a time and then ordered all locks changed and two sets of keys made, one of which he kept himself, entrusting the other to me. The disappearance of drugs stopped.

The attitude of the first surgeon had changed toward me even while I was still a nurse, and our relations had become friendly. After my appointment as pharmacist, we became intimate. Occasionally, when he had a critical case that might need prompt attention, he stayed overnight at the prison in the penthouse containing several bedrooms which was provided for such emergencies. Then he might invite me to visit him, and we would talk on many subjects. I found him a fine person whose hostile mannerisms arose largely from a war that went on within him. I remember him walking the floor, his head thrown back, talking vehemently:

"I'm an inmate of this jail as much as you are. My job here has swallowed me up and it's made me prison-minded. I want to leave, but I don't. Maybe I'm afraid. Maybe I'm just a frustrated surgeon, and I take it out on the poor devils who have to be here. What do they say about me?"

I told him as truthfully as I could what they did say, and it was not complimentary. He listened carefully and answered, "They're partly wrong, but I suppose they're right in a lot of their thinking."

I have seen that man work with a fierce intensity to save an inmate's life and then be pretty rough when his patient could stand for it. I realize now that he was suffering some of the pangs which all of us shared. We were all at war with something within ourselves.

17.

EXPLOSIONS IN POPULATION

It seemed that every member of population at one time or another stood framed in the doorway of the pharmacy for a brief moment. And each of them, as the Top Man had said, was a story in himself—a colorful one, if you had a mind to read it.

Sometimes the Top Man himself would stop on his way to the end of the corridor to take a needle bath in the hydrotherapy room. The treatment had been prescribed by a doctor, and he was given a daily pass to the hospital. He would speak in his courtly way to Boots and me and perhaps suggest that I prepare a dose of Epsom salts for him.

"On prescription only, you know," I would say.

"Certainly, certainly, the prescription. Of course, that will be attended to."

The Red Slugger came, suffering from headaches and sleeplessness, with a doctor's prescription for pills, which I filled. He had already left the dormitory in H-2 to go to F block as the champion of his faction. He had departed, striding proudly as a champion should, with sycophants to the right and left of him carrying his equipment and belongings. In his new quarters he was made much of, and he asserted himself boldly. The inevitable conflict between champions came at last. The Red Slugger gave his all, but he was only a so-so welterweight, and he had stepped out of his class. When the fray was over he was a fallen champion, and those who had coddled him deserted. As I saw him framed in the doorway, pride was no longer in him, and he drooped.

A few days later he was back again, complaining that the pills did him no good, so I gave him some little pellets of sugar with the impressive warning that he should take no more than two of them before he went to bed. He came back later for more and assured me that they were just what he needed. This time I sent him to the doctor across the corridor for a prescription; I could hear him arguing that he wanted the pills I gave him.

I stepped across to the office, and the doctor asked me, "What was it that you gave?"

"Placebo, Doctor." It was a term used for medicine dedicated to the imagination.

The doctor nodded his head gravely: "Placebo, quite right. I should have thought of that myself." He tore up his own prescription, wrote another, and gave it to me.

The potency of placebo must have worn off, for not much later the Red Slugger came to the hospital on a stretcher weltering in his own blood. He had cut his throat with a safety razor but had missed the jugular vein, and the bleeding had been stopped. While he was in the hospital I visited him, and he confided in me as if I were his manager. His confidences were almost unintelligible, for he fumbled clumsily with ideas.

I spoke to the Top Man about him. He smiled and said, "I could have written that chapter in advance. I'm going to suggest that he be sent back to H-2 where I can give him appropriate injections of ego, which will be more potent than placebo. He hasn't so much longer to go, and on the outside men are needed who have strong hands and strong backs."

He did what he proposed, and not long afterward I saw the Red Slugger in stockade with his head up, walking on the right hand of the Top Man, a half-step to the rear. Occasionally I could see him inflate his chest and harden the muscles across his shoulders, and I knew the feel of them made him proud and that again he was ready for all comers. Later still I saw him as excited as a little boy, for the day of his deliverance was at hand.

After he was gone the Top Man tossed a coin speculatively: "Fifty-fifty that he makes the grade. It all depends—the Slugger is punchy, you know, and not very bright—it all depends on his manager." Then he turned to me: "How many of these men can make the grade, do you suppose?"

I had thought of that many times myself. "It's hard to say," I replied. "They can't be classified. They come here for such a variety of causes. There's no reason why some of them can't get along with society after they get out, but some are sure to get tangled up again."

He nodded: "Quite true. Nearly half of them are here for crimes that did not exist when I was a young man. Every time a new criminal law is passed it brings a new section of society into the field of lawbreakers or likely ones. We've gone a long way beyond the Ten Commandments.

"The cross section here is only a sampling of the actual lawbreakers. Even the judges who send us all the civilian cases provide samples of their profession for our population. You may remember one famous case. The newspapers had to reassure us, saying he was the first to sell justice since Lord Bacon. I had to smile behind my hand. I've known too many of them. He was, I'm told, kept under lock and key for fear that population might tear him to pieces.

"There was another judge who nearly joined us during my time—a hung jury saved him. The boys were bitter about that. What a jury! A bunch of fools or worse. Population convicted him without a dissenting voice, on the evidence too. They didn't miss a word of the published testimony. Now there's a third judge under inquiry. Population has followed the congressional investigation, and they're way ahead of it. For them it has passed through the stage of indictment, trial, and conviction, and they drool in anticipation of his coming."

Shortly after the departure of the Red Slugger, Johnnie the nurse was also released. Everybody wished him well— even Madam Captain, though she qualified her good wishes with, "Johnnie, if you'd only grow up and be a man you'd have a chance, but I don't believe you will and I expect to see you back here again."

Johnnie laughed, "Sure, I'll be back, my Captain, to see you—I'll be longing for a good bawling out. But I'm not coming back as an inmate, not me."

It was less than two months later that the word ran through population: "Johnnie's coming back." The reason for his coming was given in picturesque detail. He had been driving a car geared for speed, with government agents chasing him. They were close on his tail when Johnnie made a short turn at a gas station and wrapped his car around a gasoline pump. Then they got him. Of course, Johnnie had protested that he didn't know that his car was loaded with contraband liquor. Everybody grinned at that part of the story; it was like Johnnie. Anyway, he had drawn a year and a day, and shortly he was in quarantine for two weeks, and then he was back in the operating room again. There Madam Captain met him, and the story of Madam's reaction went the rounds.

"So you're back again," she said to Johnnie, and then she chuckled four times—four times by actual verified count.

The Cracker from Georgia made another trip to the hospital, this time in the medical ward on the first floor where I could see him occasionally. Confinement in jail had done his general health no good, but under the care he got in the hospital he improved rapidly—so rapidly, in fact, that he became too unruly to handle and was confined in the "strip room"

174

for disciplinary purposes. The strip room, situated between the drug room and the ward, was bare of furnishings, and its occupant was stripped of his clothes. I saw him go in and was troubled, for I knew he did not tame easily. He went in one morning and was still there twenty-four hours later when I went out to visit the commissary. I got my pass from the guard sitting at the inner end of the passageway, and I asked him about his prisoner.

"He seems to be taking it all right," was his reply. "I'm thinking about recommending that he be restored to the hospital in an hour or so. Right now he's walking around, and when I spoke to him a short time ago his answers were decent enough."

The steel gate at the end of the passageway to the main corridor was open. When I returned some fifteen or twenty minutes later, I passed through the gate and was halfway down the passage when the guard rushed past me at a dead run. I backed against the wall to let him pass—a dozen strides behind him was the tall figure of a naked man taking great leaping strides. He too rushed past me. The guard got outside the gate, which he swung to and bolted.

His pursuer, brought up short, beat on the bars of the gate with a section of pipe he carried, shouting furious imprecations. While I watched, the naked one turned around, and I recognized the Cracker. I spoke to him by name in a sharp voice. At first it was clear he did not comprehend what I said. Then his expression changed, and a bewildered look came over his face.

"Come along with me," I ordered. He followed me into the corridor of the hospital and we sat down on the long bench outside the drug room. I turned to him. "Now tell me all about it." He seemed to relax and began to shiver violently. "Wait a moment. I'll get something to cover you."

I went to the door of the drug room. It was closed tight,

top and bottom. I opened it with my key. Inside was Boots his eyes staring large and white.

"What's the idea of closing up?" I said.

"Where's that wild man?" he asked.

"You mean the Cracker? He's not wild, he's outside here.' I took the coat I sometimes used when I went to stockade, and started out.

"Maybe he is all right," said Boots, "but I ain't arguing with no mad dog, and you won't find many doors open along the corridor."

I got the Cracker into the coat and started him talking. At first his story came in hysterical bursts, then it flowed in a stream. He was giving me a full explanation.

"I was mad when they put me in the strip room, but after a spell I kind of quieted down and then I remembered, 'Easy does it, easy does it,' and I kept saying that over to myself. I don't know how long I was in there—ages it seemed—and then the guard talked to me through the slit in the door and I talked nice to him. I was feelin' all right, and he said he was going to tell the Chief and I'd be out pretty soon. So I kept on saying 'Easy does it' and started walking around the cell just lazy like. Then—I can't quite remember what happened—but I know that something was walking behind me, and I walked faster and it walked faster, and then it seemed to me there wasn't enough room in the cell for both of us, and I had to do something. I had to smash something—I had to smash everything."

The pitch of his voice rose. "Easy does it," I reminded him. He paused for a moment, and I, who was facing that way, saw the guard enter the corridor, but the Cracker didn't. He carried a stout staff, and behind him were several others similarly equipped. Without changing expression I motioned to them casually with my hand. They got the signal and stepped back out of sight. The Cracker went on more quietly:

"Somehow I ripped out the radiator. I can feel it give now. The steam poured into the cell. I had this pipe in my hands. All I could think of was that I had to get out, and I did. I must've pried the door open, but I felt I had to go, and *go*. When I saw the guard I knew I hated him, and I went after him but he got away. I can remember seeing him through the gate and I can remember pounding on the steel bars. Then I began to wonder about what I was doing, and I turned around, and you spoke to me. Your voice seemed to come from way off somewhere, but when it got right near I could understand the words, and then I thought, 'Is this me or someone else?' "

We talked for a while longer. I could tell him honestly that I understood, that it had almost happened to me once. When he seemed quieted I walked down the corridor with him—his long shanks showed under the tail of my coat. We entered the second strip room, which was furnished with a cot. I got him to lie down on it, and I covered him with the coat. He went to sleep almost immediately.

When I went out I told the guard, "I think he'll be all right when he wakes up. Let me know when he does, and I'll go in to see him. He's not a bad fellow."

The guard looked dubious and grunted, "When I saw him coming out of the strip room with that piece of pipe in his hand and the steam pouring out after him, he looked to me like something let out of hell." Then he grinned. "I never thought I could love a steel-barred gate the way I love that one."

The Cracker's explosion had fallen just short of grim tragedy, but there was another incident in population which carried to the ultimate. The little German sailor whom I had known in quarantine was its central figure. I had seen him from time to time, but he never talked to me. In fact, so far as I could observe, he talked to no one except in monosyllables. He must have broken his rule on at least one occasion, for he and the man known as the Killer had come to blows over a difference of opinion concerning an announcement on the bulletin board about the progress of the war. Both were brought to the hospital, the Killer with a puncture wound in the abdomen which responded to treatment, the sailor with a broken skull. He had been dragged by the feet down the concrete steps of his cell block, and the back of his head was badly crushed.

He lingered some ten days without regaining consciousness, and died. I saw him on the slab in the morgue. He looked pathetically small; most of us do when we linger and die. I said a silent prayer over him. I thought of those in his native land who perhaps were looking forward to the day when he would return to them, and here he was lying in a strange place, in a strange land, where his death caused nothing but a buzz of excited conversation which then faded out like a ripple on a pond.

With fifteen or sixteen hundred men confined under the unnatural conditions of a jail, each thrown back on his own resources, each centered on himself, extraordinary things happen and extraordinary ideas germinate and grow into unexpected forms. My experience in solitary confinement had enabled me to understand the incredible accomplishments of prisoners who tunnel great distances with instruments so utterly inadequate and by steps so infinitesimal that their patience passes belief. Escape may be the underlying urge, but the necessity of having a purpose in life is the thing that keeps them at it.

The same necessity leads to other plans for escape which are remarkable less for patience than for their reckless disregard of the odds against them. I became familiar with one attempt involving three men. I knew them all, and on the day their plan culminated in action, I had seen them sitting on the bench in the corridor of the hospital. They had come on special passes to see the Chief. I saw them file into his office. Two were relative newcomers with sentences not exceeding five years. The third was a long-termer known throughout population, already an old inhabitant though still young, a handsome dark fellow who carried himself erect and was quick in his step and movements. Once he had broken out of a state jail and had made his exploit melodramatic by kidnapping the warden's wife in his getaway. There was an air of reckless daring about him, and an assurance that attracted a following. Of him the Top Man had said, "He has a quick mind that snaps at a glittering idea and is hooked. You can't get him off the hook. Already he's accumulated a record that will wreck any chance for parole, and someday he'll be caught by another idea that will get him extra time and Alcatraz."

After seeing the three enter the Chief's office, I had gone to the surgical ward; the subsequent events were told to me later. The doctor's secretary had been expecting them, and she directed the long-termer to the doctor's office. The other two remained with her awaiting their turn. Presently the doctor came out followed by his patient. To her horror the secretary saw a knife held at the doctor's back. In an even voice the doctor ordered her to say nothing and to fall in behind, which she did, flanked by the other two inmates. In that formation the procession moved out of the hospital through the passageway into the main corridor, past the hospital guard and a guard in the main corridor, thence through two more gates at

179

the entrance to the hallway of the administration building, past a guard at its front door, and then out of the main prison building. They crossed the belt of lawn to the tower at the main entrance, gained admission to the tower, and stood at the great door which would let them outside of the prison walls. There they stopped; the door could be opened only by the guard in the gallery halfway up the rear wall of the tower.

Just what happened then was never made clear. Perhaps in the excitement no one quite knew, but the guard in the gallery saw the knife. He couldn't believe his eyes. Then the melee began, during which a tear bomb exploded, and the doctor and his secretary got loose. There was a brief spell of fighting and a frenzy of blows, and the three were overcome. The alarm was given, the terrifying wail of the siren flooded the jail, all inmates except those on the hospital staff were sent hurrying to their respective cells or dormitories to be locked in, and the question haunted the air, "What does it mean?"

From the sun porch of the surgical ward where I stood we could see the three would-be escapees being herded by half a dozen guards along the walk just inside the prison wall. The guards were overwrought—at the least sign of loitering or stumbling the prisoners were beaten with clubs. Occasionally they fell and were beaten as they lay. It was a sickening sight, but we watched fascinated until the group disappeared under the hospital wall en route to the Hole.

A thing like that just couldn't happen; yet it did. Each guard was under orders to permit no inmate to go through a gate without a pass, but three of them had. They were disciplined for it, and they could merely mutter, "It was the Chief, so we let him pass. Who could have thought such a thing possible?" Moreover, prisoners could not have knives. That was against orders which were so vigilantly enforced that mattresses were examined with special equipment, but here was

180

a knife loose in population. There were a dozen other reasons why the whole scheme was preposterous, but nothing about it was more preposterous than the degree to which it had worked.

The ringleader of that little group drew his extra time—more than two men could serve—and when able to be moved he was swallowed up in Alcatraz. Perhaps he had figured that he had nothing to lose and that the thrill of the gamble was worth the price he paid. The other two young fellows who had followed him, fascinated, also suffered.

The excitement in the jail was intense. The story flew throughout population. The fantastic nature of the attempt and the brutal beatings were matters that heated men's minds. There was a surge of restlessness, nerves tightened, and the younger men moved about ready to leap into action at a touch. The guards, conscious of the tension, watched everyone everywhere, alert for what might happen. It was a full week before the prison relaxed and became itself again.

I had noticed much the same feeling in our prison when the outbreak at Alcatraz made news. The spirit of that rebellion had entered our own walls, and for at least a week it seemed that something would burst out among us. A prison outbreak anywhere starts waves vibrating which produce sympathetic responses thousands of miles away.

18.

'THE TERRIBLE MEEK'

In January, 1943, about three months after moving into H-block, I left the dormitory for an individual cell in J-block, which was at the western end of the main corridor farthest removed from the hospital. The conscientious objector known as the Kid had gone ahead of me. It troubled him, apparently, that I had been deprived of his guardianship, and he urged me to join him. I applied for transfer and received permission to change quarters. "My cloistered cell and monastic seclusion," as I referred to it in my letters, was a marked change from the confusion of the smoke-filled dormitory where many visitors sought me out, sat on the edge of my cot, and discussed the subject that concerned them.

My new cell in J-2 was No. 228, which touched off a homesick memory, for the street number of my parsonage had also been 228. In the cell next to me was the Kid. Our cell doors were not locked, for J-2 was an "honor block." At night, however, the steel-barred gate at the entrance was closed and bolted. The seclusion of my new quarters gave me an opportunity to read, and I note in my letters references to the books I secured from the library, which comprise a formidable catalogue ranging from Goethe's *Faust* (a translation by Bayard Taylor, which I thought on the whole well done) through Schweitzer's *Life and Thoughts* and *The Life of Michelangelo* translated from the French, to Booth Tarkington's stories and *The Yearling*.

The Kid was also a reader. He dug into the most formidable authors, including Kant and Spinoza, and was eager to discuss with me new ideas and new slants acquired in the course of his reading. He had been assigned to a teaching job in the educational department on the second floor of the administration building. The subjects he taught were English for the foreign-speaking population (most of them Italians) and elementary reading and writing, for which he had a surprisingly large number of pupils.

He performed his duties with a conscientiousness that was in accord with his concept of living. When he entered population he had met insult and contempt, for patriotism there was equal to that outside the walls and was quicker to find expression. Conscientious objectors were considered slackers and cowards, and they had to convince their fellows to the contrary. Some succeeded, some did not. Those whose main concern was to make their stay as easy as possible were held in low esteem, but those who took what came without complaint, carried themselves simply, and were ready to help others unselfishly acquired the grudging respect of both population and the administration.

The Kid met the qualifications and was respected. Helping others he counted as a duty, and he was ready to give unstintingly of himself and his meager possessions. The confidence of the administration in him was manifested when he was placed outside the walls in the barracks where the Mennonites, Dunkards, Amish, and similar pacifist sects were quartered. He worked with them on the farm until he was sent to the hospital with a severe attack of eczema, and he did not go back.

Among certain of the conscientious objectors the Kid had considerable influence. It was shown not by any attempt at leadership on his part but by the way he affected the others in setting them an example. The group to which he himself belonged was a noncohesive one made up of individualists who included Christians, both white and Negro, and some Jews. Many of these recognized their kinship to the Quakers, the foundation of their convictions being much the same.

The other groups—the Pennsylvania Dutch pacifist sects, of whom we saw little within the walls, and the Jehovah's Witnesses—stood apart. The Jehovah's Witnesses had their new and virile religion to hold them together. They were difficult to talk to, for each was an apostle of a faith which compelled him, he felt, to preach, and each was armed with an assortment of texts lifted from the Bible. With these he would bombard his listeners in a spirit that seemed to say, "Accept the words of Holy Writ or your soul will be lost." My own more philosophical interpretation of the Word was impatiently brushed aside as sophistication; I often felt as if I were in the presence of primitive Christianity as it existed fifteen centuries ago after the Western church divorced itself from the learning of the East.

The Kid was one of those people who will hold stubbornly to a cause they feel to be righteous. I knew him, and I knew that his drawn, gaunt face was the product of a struggle that went on within him. He was no "slacker"; his convictions against war called for self-sacrifice equivalent to what he might suffer in war. I watched him and wondered what form the sacrifice would take. Now and again some prisoner's difficulty would strike him forcefully as resulting from injustice, and he would ask for an interview with the assistant warden whose duty it was to hear complaints; there he would plead the other man's cause, usually without that man's knowledge.

It was some time near the end of the year 1943 when the guard assigned to our block asked me into his office. He told me that the Kid had asked for and had received permission to interview the assistant warden the following day to discuss the parole of conscientious objectors. The guard saw it this way:

"There's no sense in the interview. He'll be turned down, of course. They can't be paroled. Wouldn't it make a fine fuss to have these C.O.'s walking around a town where most of the boys are at war? What I wish you would do is persuade him to lay off the idea. I'm afraid there's trouble in it."

I agreed to try, but expressed no confidence of success. It was just the kind of cause that would grip the Kid. He would have no personal interest in the result of the interview, for paroled prisoners were required to sign a list of pledges, which he had resolved never to do. But we had our discussion that night. I defended the administration on the grounds mentioned by the guard, which seemed reasonable to me. But he replied that conscientious objectors were violators of the law; since they were jailed and treated as other violators, they should receive the same privileges. At that point the argument was deadlocked. The following evening he told me that the interview had taken place and that he hoped it would bear fruit.

I got the full story of the interview from the clerk to the assistant warden, a banker from the South who was doing twenty-five years for conspiracy to rob his own bank. He too had a cell in our block, but he had been there for years. In doing his time he had sealed off the part of him that was bitter and frustrated, and he moved about quietly and cautiously as if he were afraid of breaking the seal. But the Kid's interview gave him the urge to talk, so he visited me in the evening and sat on the steel chair in my room and told me about it while I sat on the edge of the cot. It was a pleasure to listen to him. I liked the inflection of his voice and the elusive humor that clung to his words, which can only be approximated here:

"I was sitting at my desk with the door open into my chief's office when the Kid came in. His approach, I assure you, was impeccable, displaying respect for authority to the point of submissiveness. On invitation he sat down and faced the Awful Presence. You know how awful the Presence is—how massively stern, how he looks at you while the seconds go by ticking with the beat of your heart, and then his voice, heavy and rasping, bearing down upon you. I tell you, my boss has his technique; when he speaks, he is master of the situation. So he told the Kid off. Told him the administration's position. It was an old story. It seemed to beat the Kid down. He was meek, and then he started to talk so quietly and hesitantly that it seemed ungracious to cut him off.

"His argument was an old story too but without your noticing where it happened he gave it a new twist, and he was talking of the jail as a monstrous place where human beings, creatures with souls, were caged like beasts and other men were their keepers. As he talked, the crime of the keepers began to overshadow the crimes of the kept. A warden's job was a shameful thing. At the finish he was urging the warden to forsake his job before it destroyed his immortal soul and to flee this place as the warned fled Sodom and Gomorrah.

"And would you believe me?" the Banker went on after a pause, "the Kid had *me* convinced, and that tough-grained boss of mine, who wears his job like a decoration, was put on the defensive. He found himself apologizing for being a warden, and, what's more, it seemed only natural for him to do so. Then the Kid got up and departed, as respectful as when he had come in. It was quite a while before I came to and recognized the grotesque humor of the interview—and at about the same time my boss began to grunt and fume about the position he had been put in. He prides himself on taking and holding the upper hand, and the Kid had taken the play away from him."

186

The Banker paused for a moment while he balanced himself on the hind legs of the chair; then he came down on all four gently: "Do you know what keeps running through my mind? It's that biblical text, 'Blessed are the meek: for they shall inherit the earth.' You can check me if I have it wrong. It comes out of an old spot in my memory. When I first learned it, I was young and I worried about it. It didn't seem to me to make sense as it was written, and I wondered whether it had some hidden meaning. Now I suspect maybe it's right as it is." He stopped again, then went on, "The terrible meek, the terrible meek—that Kid can cause more trouble for the management in this jail than the toughest fellow in population."

I doubt if the Banker told this story to many others and I know I didn't, but as usual almost everyone in population knew it at once. For them it was a good story with a satisfying twist. The prisoners resented the "ruling class," and the Kid had asserted the equality of those down under. So the story went the rounds until it was worn out. It was almost as gratifying as the story that had come out of the kitchen the time the cook and his crew fouled the coffee for the officers' mess.

But the interview effected no change in parole policy. The Kid remained quiescent for a number of months. He was obviously brooding. Then—and again it was the guard who broke the news—the Kid had served notice that he would not report for work the next morning. He was determined to protest the fact that no action had been taken on his proposition; and he had a further protest, one that always had been debated extensively, against the segregation of the white and the colored prisoners.

The guard spoke to me as I passed his quarters. This time he seemed gravely troubled. If the Kid defied orders a penalty would have to be imposed. He considered himself a reasonable guard, capable of getting co-operation without cracking down, so he asked for my aid. I was likewise troubled. I did not wish to see the Kid offer himself up as a sacrifice for a lost cause. I felt that his plan was pure folly, but I knew that was no argument. But I tried, and tried earnestly. The Kid admitted readily enough that he was challenging the forces of the administration singlehanded, that he could expect to suffer severely for it; but his decision was the result of a long struggle within himself, and he was willing to accept the consequences, even death, and I knew he was not indulging in dramatics.

Again we went over the arguments on the parole question, and then turned to the matter of segregation. I told him, "I hope I'm as ready as anyone to recognize the qualities that make a man no matter what group I find him in, but that does not blind me to the facts—facts that show here in jail. We can all see how uneasy is the line that separates the races and how readily bloodshed can start." I brought up an incident of not long before when a white inmate in the carpenter's shop struck a Negro on the head with a hammer.

The story was that the Negro was a pervert and had attempted assault. It was a reasonable story, for the Negro's character was known. If he had been white, population would have shrugged its shoulders, called him a coarse name, and returned a verdict of "good riddance." But he was a Negro, and the Negro inmates were troubled, and the tension between the groups was aggravated. The guards were increased at crucial locations and became more vigilant, but with all their vigilance trouble broke out once in the corridor. It was suppressed, but a dozen men were carried to the hospital. Other fights had broken out in the dining room and other places of contact. The matter was not one of theory but of experience. Maybe the tension between the groups would disappear if there were no segregation, but if in making the test one or a dozen men were killed, certainly the men who assumed responsibility for the experiment would bear the blame.

He was ready enough with his answer. He saw in his plan a great purpose, one that should be carried out even if it entailed a grave hazard. He was satisfied that segregation caused the tension. If it were terminated, the tension would disappear. Any trouble that arose would not persist.

There was nothing left for me to do but make a personal appeal. Would he hold back his protest out of regard for me? He considered that appeal seriously but concluded by telling me that he had thought the matter over for many months before determining to act. He would make any personal sacrifice for me (which I knew to be true), but in this instance he would be sacrificing others, and that he had no right to do.

Perhaps you may think him a perverse sort of fool. I concede that I fretted over his obduracy. I thought his proposal futile and certain to bring suffering upon him, but I restrained any display of temper and quieted my disturbed feelings; we talked of other things.

The Kid did not go to work in the morning. Later in the day he was sent down the corridor toward the assistant warden's office, but at the prison captain's desk he was stopped and told to sit on the bench along the wall. There he sat with neither food nor drink for two days and well into a third. Nobody could speak to him. Population marched by, some callous, some sneering, and some deeply troubled. I had to pass him a number of times, and I suffered with him. I could see the lines deepening in his face and his eyes sinking deeper in their sockets, his clothes shriveling about him as his body shrank in size. He came to look like a mummy, all teeth and bone—a mummy supernaturally alive, its life showing only in its stricken eyes; finally, that evidence of life failed too, and he was carried off a collapsed, inanimate bundle, piteously small. He was revived by injections in the hospital and given water, but he refused to eat and in a few days was removed to a solitary confinement cell in A-block. There the cells are in a double row back to back; their fronts are steel bars, behind which there is no privacy.

But the Kid did not go alone. Beginning with the second day of his martyrdom, it was reported that other conscientious objectors had also served notice that they would refuse to comply with orders; they too went to A-block. They would drink water but refused to eat. Some others worked and even went to the dining room, but they refused to eat; when they were too weak to carry on, they also were transferred to A-block.

The Swede had a perplexing problem. He was a valuable aide in the operating room. His services were particularly necessary to others. He refused to eat for four days, until he had become so affected he could not do his work properly; then he had to make a choice of his primary duty. He chose to eat and serve, and I think he determined wisely. I never doubted that under other circumstances he would have gone through to the bitter end. There were others who refused to eat at first but gave up after three or four days.

For ten days it was impossible to tell how far the contagion would spread. No Jehovah's Witnesses took part, and of the pacifist sects only the Quakers joined in. On the tenth day twenty-two C.O.'s were in solitary confinement, and this was the high-water mark of the movement. Twenty-two young men were ultimately carried into the hospital, shrunken and feeble but still resolute; they were strapped to their cots, and I prepared a liquid mixture with a glucose base which was fed to them through a tube inserted into the nostrils. It was not an appetizing sight.

Several of them were affected to the point where they had

to be transferred as mental cases to individual rooms on the hospital's second floor. They seemed tractable enough and were freed of their straps, but they were locked in at night. For the unbalanced imagination of one man the ordeal was too much; one morning there was a bloodstain under his door, and he was found dead on the floor with slashed wrists.

I do not recall just how long we kept the others alive by force-feeding, but it seems to me that I prepared the glucose solution for weeks. Then, after negotiations with the administration in the course of which some sort of assurances were given, the hunger strike ended and our recalcitrant charges recovered.

The whole thing seemed utterly unreasonable, and yet it had been built upon virtues that we usually rate highly— devotion to a cause and the willingness to sacrifice oneself for it. Of course, we are likely to discount the virtue as perverseness if we do not approve of the cause, but that is a mere play on words. To me those boys showed something that commanded my admiration. However fantastic their idea might have been, they skirted death for it and, I have no doubt, were willing to accept death itself.

The affair caused the administration grave concern and resulted in daily consultations with Washington. The conscientious objectors must not be permitted to defy rules, and yet they should not be permitted to die. Then the anxiety arose as to how far the influence of their example would reach. It might spread like a contagion and affect the whole jail with insubordination. Daily reports went to Washington on the growth of the movement up to that point when it began to subside—and what a relief that must have been!

Whenever I thought of those boys, the words of the Banker ran through my mind like a refrain: "The terrible meek, the terrible meek."

It was some time later that the hospital psychologist, with

191

whom my relations were by this time close and friendly, spoke to me of a case in the mental ward that was baffling both him and the psychiatrist. Another conscientious objector, a young man, had been transferred from the institution at Danbury. He had been carried in on a stretcher, having eaten nothing for a considerable period of time and being too weak to stand. He seemed determined to die. The doctors had interviewed him several times, and he had answered their queries dutifully enough. But they could not break his fixation on death. It was suggested that I might be able to do something with him, and I agreed to try.

When I entered the young fellow's room, he was lying very still and was so aloof it seemed as if his spirit had already entered another world. His appearance, with his arms partly spread out, made me think of someone lying upon a cross. I sat quietly on the chair by his bedside watching him. The bones of his face showed through skin that was thin and fragile like papier-maché; his hair was unkempt, and where it grew down his cheeks and sprayed out in a thin beard over his throat it was crinkly and red. It must have been my uniform which drew his attention at last, for he asked in a faint voice if I were a doctor.

I shook my head. "No, I am an inmate like yourself." I noticed that there was a Bible on top of his locker. I opened it and read from the eighth chapter of Paul's Epistle to the Romans. The pale eyes were fixed on me, and when I finished the voice came again.

"Who are you?"

"That," I said, "I would rather not tell you. Some people think me a very evil person. You can find out about me from any of your nurses. I shall come back tomorrow. If you want to talk to me then, I shall be pleased."

When I came the next day, he said he had heard my story

and wished me to stay. So I talked to him at some length and pointed out that there was nothing unique in his being imprisoned for his faith. The history of the Christian church led through many prisons. His pacifist belief I might not share, but I could respect it. However, he should be prepared to suffer for his faith. It is sometimes easier to die than to live. I myself more than once had wished that death might come, but to bring it upon oneself did not show Christian fortitude. Our faith forbids us to despair. Moreover, he did not live for himself alone. He had a wife and child whom he loved and who needed him. What he was now called upon to endure was beyond his power to change. He must submit and let God's will be done.

I supplemented my remarks by reading from his Bible. He followed me attentively, uttering a word or two only now and then, and I could feel that his will to live had revived. When it came time for me to leave he assured me he would try to live, so I released his straps. Though he had gone near to the edge of death, his recovery was rapid, and in a week he could be moved to quarantine. Eventually he was assigned to work in the greenhouse, where flowers were raised within the prison walls, an assignment appropriate to his vocation in the outside world. I talked the case over later with the psychologist. It was clear that the young fellow had been confused to the point of hopelessness by the clash of his beliefs with the mandate of society. To him the clash seemed to mean the end of all things. His confusion was increased by the psychological approach. All I had done was to clarify his thinking by presenting the principles and texts of the faith he followed.

The pacifist sectarians of German background were readily identifiable when they entered jail from the outside world by their plain dark clothes hanging straight and loose, their broad-brimmed black hats, and their uncut hair and beards. The sun porch of the surgical ward faced south, and from it we could look across to the tower that surmounted the entrance gate and see the new arrivals come through its inner door just as all of us had entered, and watch them being directed along the cement walk along the foot of the wall, across the green strip, and down into the receiving room.

When these people entered they were submissive—we had all been submissive, but there was a quality in their submission which seemed to say, "You may do what you will with my body, but my spirit is mine and I shall keep it inviolate." They offered no resistance to orders to strip for examination, or to the prison garb they were required to wear, or to the shaves and haircuts given by a prison barber. To this defilement of their bodies they were indifferent. They accepted their quarters in the farm dormitory, outside of the walls but still within the prison grounds, and performed their duties on the farm without instruction or urging. In their faith the good earth and its fruits were God's gifts and were to be cared for as such.

We saw little of them in population. They came to sick call with the other trusties from outside the wall at special hours on Wednesdays and Sundays, and I met them briefly while handing over their prescriptions at the pharmacy door.

Later I came to know two of them, members of the Mennonite sect, when they were brought to the hospital for operations. They occupied a room where I had occasion to visit them. At first they paid little heed to me and lay very still as if in contemplation. The older of the two had a Bible opened at his bedside, printed in double columns of English and German. I spoke to him in the Pennsylvania Dutch dialect, and the sound of the familiar words aroused his interest. He looked at me in surprise and replied in the same language.

"You speak as we speak. How can that be?"

So I told him enough of my story to explain, and he did not press the inquiry but seemed content with the opportunity to converse in his own dialect. I visited them a number of times and on occasion read from the German text of their Bible. They came to accept me as a friend. In none of the conversations did they complain of what had happened to them. *God had willed it so*. But the older man took me into his confidence and revealed some of his thoughts on the subject.

He and his people had come to Pennsylvania more than two centuries ago when it lay at the fringe of the known world to live in peace with God. They cared for the good earth and the earth took care of them. It was His earth and He made it fruitful. They lived as they believed God willed they should live. Now the world with its bloodshed and strife had once again come upon them. They would have to journey in search of a new place where they might worship God and do his bidding. I wondered where that place might be, and he seemed to sense my question.

"Perhaps there is no such place," he said quietly. "That we shall accept as His will. If we are destroyed, that too we must accept, but we shall abide in our faith. It can be only our bodies that are destroyed, and all must come to that end. Our spirits will remain with Him."

His plight troubled me then and still troubles me. I knew his people, and I regarded them highly. They are not soft. They are rugged, they have strong wills, they do not spare themselves, and they perform great labors. Of course, they can be earthy, but those I speak of here had a simple purity of character which appeared to me beautiful when sublimated by the fire of suffering. I am sure there are many such among their people. We create an image of Tolerance with a benign countenance; the face it turns toward them is the horrid face of Medusa.

19.

THE SHORT AND THE LONG

To one who has lived in the penitentiary for a few days or for a few weeks, population seems a static pool confined within four walls, but after a residence of a few years, the concept changes. The pool is continually discharging into and being replenished from the outside world, though its level remains constant at fifteen to seventeen hundred men, both inmates and staff. When I arrived at Lewisburg the prison was eleven years old, and I was inmate number 12150. About two and half years later I noticed the low fifteen thousands appearing as inmates' numbers on the prescriptions presented at the drug room.

Each prisoner, upon being committed, is given a slip of paper bearing the date of his commitment and other dates vitally important to him. I received such a slip when I first entered Danbury, containing merely the date of my commitment. I received another slip when I returned to Danbury after sentence, and when I entered Lewisburg I received a third slip in the following form:

Sentence Notice to Inmates
Department of Justice
Penal and Correctional Institutions
U.S. Northeast Penitentiary

Lewisburg, September 24, 1942

To Kurt Emil Bruno Molzahn   12150

According to commitment papers filed in your case

you were sentenced August 25, 1942, to a term of
ten years   months   days.
You were received at the Danbury Penitentiary
August 25, 1942.
Your sentence begins August 25, 1942.
You are eligible for parole December 24, 1945.
Your "good conduct" term expires May 12, 1949.
Your full term expires August 24, 1952.
Good time allowed 1200 days.

(Official)

_____

Recording Clerk

Keep this notice in good condition in your cell until
the date of your release from the penitentiary.

For those whose terms were a year and a day, the date of
eligibility for parole was only four months removed from the
date of sentence and the "good conduct" term expired at the
end of eight months. When I looked at mine and then thought
of theirs, I could understand the contempt of the long-termers
for short-termers who seemed to be here today and gone tomorrow.

The parole board, consisting of three members whose head-
quarters were in Washington, traveled the circuit of the federal
prisons. At Lewisburg it appeared quarterly, in January, April,
July, and October, when it gave hearings to those who were or
would shortly become eligible for parole as well as to others
who had failed earlier and whose cases were up for recon-
sideration.

The coming of the board excited great interest among those
who would be called before it, and intense emotions were
evoked. Approximately one in five would make parole, and
the problem was how to become the lucky fifth. In a letter I
wrote of the jail, "It is a city of stone and steel built upon a

soil where rumors grow along with hopes—many dreamers live in this exclusive city." Many of the rumors, hopes, and dreams centered on the parole board. There was discussion of what one should say and how one should act in order to influence the board, and there were dark rumors about what connections one needed to accomplish that end. The names of lawyers, congressmen, and other public officials were debated as to the "pull" each one might exercise on the board. During my time one particular congressman had the top rating. If you got him, you were as good as sprung. However, since those who made parole always refused to discuss the matter, perhaps out of fear of its revocation before the release date, there was really no authentic information available about what influenced the board's action.

Apparently the board members were courteous to those who came before them and sometimes made compliments about a man's prison record. Such remarks buoyed hopes, and the longer they were mulled over the more significant they would appear and the more assured a prisoner would feel of favorable action; then, when in the face of his confidence the answer was "Parole denied," a man was plunged into black despair. It may readily be understood that the shadow of the parole board hung always over population and played a major part in its life.

To a long-termer a sentence of ten years was short; nevertheless, it was substantially longer than the average sentence of the Lewisburg prisoner. Thus I saw many of the men I had come to know go out either on parole or at the expiration of their "good conduct" term.

The Rabbi was eligible for parole when the board met in October of 1943. He had anticipated his hearing before the board with an eagerness he made no attempt to conceal. He could talk and think of nothing else for days on end; during that long period of suspense—sometimes several months—which intervened between the hearing and the handing down of the board's decision, he importuned everybody—inmates, guards, prison parole officers, and the prison staff. He even insisted on seeing the warden and did so with such pertinacity that he was granted an interview in which to plead for sympathy and help. He wrote a prodigious number of letters (which may or may not have been delivered) to the board, presenting with argument and entreaties aspects of his case which he was afraid might have been overlooked at the hearing. Sometimes he wept when he talked with me about his case, but his weeping was no evidence of softening. It merely emphasized the intensity of his will. At last the notice came on December 8. It read, "Parole granted," effective December 18 unless revoked for cause.

The Rabbi was transformed at once into a briskly exuberant bundle of activity. He went about showing the notice to everybody, but in response to the eager inquiries about how he had gotten it he said nothing. With ten days to go he was taking no chances. On December 17 he visited me in the pharmacy to say goodbye. His spirits were high; "Mummy and the children" were waiting for him. I saw him last as he marched away from the drug room door with his funny strut. I hope his reception matched his expectations. Population laughed at his looks and his mannerisms, but he had a capacity for concentration of purpose that made him a unique and significant personality.

The Postmaster had received notice of the granting of his parole at the same time as the Rabbi, although his hearing had been held earlier, in July; the first report on his case had stated that action had been deferred. I saw him nearly every day, for he was a clerk in the administration office of the hospital next door to the drug room. He was never a cordial man, and his residence in the jail had thrown him more than ever back upon himself. He moved in an atmosphere of tall, gaunt reserve which enabled him to live in dormitory H-3 and still remain as separate from his fellows as if he were in a private cell. He included me among his very few friends. He received his first discomfiting notice from the board without any display of emotion, but I who knew him sensed his feeling. He received the notice that his parole had been granted with the same apparent calm, but again I knew the intensity of his thanksgiving. His plans had already been made. His wife had continued to live in the same town they had lived in before, and she had supported herself and her daughter by working as a waitress. Now they would forget that town and go to some part of the country not less than a thousand miles away where they could start over again together.

When we had talked of his case and the future he envisioned, he told me with real emotion how sad he felt at leaving me in this place and said he would hope and pray for my deliverance. He assured me, "I am not by nature an optimistic man, but I have a deep conviction that you will not serve out your sentence." Then he was gone, and his departure depressed my spirits. I could think of no way I could be released in less than six and a third years, at the end of my "good conduct" term.

Boots went out early in 1944 at the end of his "good conduct" term. He was greatly excited by the prospect of his release—so much so that he almost wrecked his chances. It was his duty to pick up bottles throughout the hospital, load them into a bag, and bring them back to pharmacy. On the day before he was to go out, he tossed the bag of bottles on the floor and broke them all. I reported officially that it had been due to nervous excitement, though I suspected an element of wilfulness. It was his last chance to get even with the hateful things that had haunted his dreams. He left me that day with a grin on his face and a cheery hope that we would meet again in the outside world.

In his place I had a new colored fellow named John. He was short and heavily muscled, and his voice was a deep bass that rumbled when he caught the pitch of the room. On Sundays he was a member of the choir and sang mightily.

Not long after Boots's departure the moving-picture magnate came to the end of his "good conduct" term. He had been a daily visitor to the hospital for insulin injections and other medications. In the outside world he must have lived largely on drugs, for when he entered prison he brought with him two large medicine cases which the guard, overwhelmed by his reputed millions, helped him carry until a superior officer interfered with the curt observation that the hospital would provide all that was necessary. He certainly put the hospital to the proof. Our relationship was friendly, and he stopped at the door of the drug room the day before he was to go out. He was as frail and wrinkled as ever, but he had an assurance about him now that somehow made him imposing. We shook hands and he invited me to visit him at his estate.

"Suppose we make it a date," I suggested. "Labor Day, eight years from this coming one."

He looked at me a little startled, perhaps wondering where he might be then, and said hastily, "Don't be so pessimistic. It won't be that long."

The next day he was gone, but the story lingered behind that when he stepped out of the prison gate he vanished into a great limousine, as Elijah vanished into the cloud.

In my cell block there were some changes and others were contemplated. The Baron had taken a cell in J-2. Prison experience had changed him not a whit. The rules of our honor block required standing just outside the cell door for the regular count. He insisted that he could be counted as well within the cell as standing like a sentry at its entrance, so I was asked by the guard to use my good offices in the matter. There was really nothing mean about the Baron. His time was "getting short" and I used the old argument about looking at the situation from the guard's point of view; it had worked once before and it worked again. He was utterly contemptuous of the rule but magnanimously waived his feelings in the matter.

The Baron's appeal had long since been disposed of against him, but he had taken the news without a whimper, just as he later accepted a denial of parole. He went out at the end of his "good conduct" term sometime in the first quarter of 1944, and I could picture his resilient figure striding out of the prison gate, his head carried as arrogantly as ever. Prison had made no noticeable impression on his character. I suppose he shed it without a backward glance. I heard afterwards that the government released his money, so perhaps he again became the millionaire playboy.

Joe's Doctor, who also had a cell in J-2, was doing fifteen years. At the end of ten he went out on "good conduct" and softened far enough at the finish to wish me well as he said goodbye. The Rabbi had tried to bring us together, but was unsuccessful. On one occasion he proposed a chess game, to which I agreed, but Joe's Doctor conditioned his acceptance upon my renouncing Hitler and Nazism. I refused to do this; my differences with Hitler and Nazism were my own affair, and I bought no man's favor. Later we did meet without conditions, and I found him a far better player than I. When he left, he entered a world different from any I had ever known. I believe he is functioning in it somewhere, perhaps in a perfectly prosaic way, but I cannot divorce him in my own mind from the strange and secretive.

A new inmate doctor of a very different sort had come into

the hospital. He was a chiropractor who had been assigned to carry on his vocation in the clinic at the end of the corridor beyond the drug room. A tall, stringy fellow with powerful arms and extraordinarily strong hands, he had a blond complexion and an open blue-eyed look in which there was something of a boy who would never grow up. He was given to sudden and violent impulses which, in view of his great strength, could make him dangerous. His title in population was "The Bone-Breaker of Break Neck Road." The source of the first part was obvious; the second grew out of the rumor that he lived on a road of that name in the outside world. He was doing three years for giving registrants for the draft pills which operated upon the action of the heart. He told me about it.

"Every one of the guys I gave pills to had asthma or said he had, and that's what the pills were for." He passed over the fact that he had no license to dispense drugs. "Then one day two of my patients came back, flashed badges, and showed a warrant for my arrest. That was a dirty trick. It made me mad so I knocked one of them kicking, pushed the other out, and bundled his buddy after him. I think I had a right to get mad. It didn't hurt 'em much, but they made an awful stew about it in court and the judge gave me three years."

His impulses got him into trouble in prison. One evening a colored fellow was brought unconscious to the emergency clinic from the indoor stockade with a badly cut mouth, broken teeth, and a bloody scalp wound. Since no doctors were on hand, I treated him, shaving his scalp and applying alcohol to the wound (which revived him sharply), then bandaging it in the approved fashion. By the time I finished I had another patient, the Bone-Breaker, with a badly lacerated right hand. I made no comment, merely giving the necessary treatment. But there were plenty who had seen the affair. What started it I do not know; there was only one blow struck, a very effective right-hand punch. The Bone-Breaker was given a hearing and sentenced to the Hole.

The doctors had authority to order the release of prisoners from the Hole, so when the young staff doctor across the way from me made his rounds, the Bone-Breaker entered a plea: "For God's sake, Doc, get me out of this damn place."

But the doctor shook his head: "No, you can just sweat it out." The Bone-Breaker remembered.

Some time after the Bone-Breaker's release the young doctor had a bad back which was causing him much discomfort. With some misgivings he decided to try a chiropractic treatment. I watched him go down the corridor to the clinic and shortly saw him coming back. He explained, "He told me I could just sweat it out." Later I visited the Bone-Breaker and talked him into a more reasonable frame of mind, and he gave the treatment. After the doctor returned to his office I stepped across to inquire how he felt and found him sitting limply in his chair.

"Did he fix you up?"

He grinned a bit painfully. "Yes," he said, "I rather think he cured me of what ailed me, but I doubt if I'll ever recover from the treatment."

I made new acquaintances in J-2. One, in the cell across from mine, was a tall, well-built young fellow doing twenty-five years for a holdup. The gang had crossed the state line in a stolen car, making theirs a federal offense, and they were all captured. Now, having done ten years of his time, he was twenty-nine years old but with a face still so youthful that it could be readily understood why his old nickname "Baby Face" persisted. But there was something vigorously masculine and forthright about him that I liked. Recently he had become a nurse in the hospital, so I saw him frequently during my working hours as well as in the cell block.

I suppose his pretty face and the reaction of others toward it had been an important factor in getting him into trouble originally and in dictating the kind of language he used. He must have wanted to convince the world that he was no sissy but a he-man and a tough guy. His language was more than profane; it was vile. One day I spoke to him about it. I told him that his words did not hurt me, since I was no sensitive flower and had heard plenty of tough talk in my time. But the words he used and the way he used them made it clear that they held no meaning to him. He would help himself, I was sure, if he used everyday speech for everyday purposes and used the tough stuff only when he needed it. If he did not want to go that far with me, he might cut out just the vile stuff and stick to profanity. I concluded, "I know you and I like you, and the language you use does not fit the kind of fellow you are."

He took my little lecture in good spirit, made an effort to speak in a more normal way, and succeeded to a marked degree. When he slipped into the old groove in my presence and became conscious of it he would turn to me with his engaging smile: "See, Reverend, the old tongue doesn't learn new tricks in a hurry."

His nursing duties were on the second floor of the hospital among the mental cases, where his forthrightness was a real help. A too-sympathetic approach sometimes did more harm than good there. He was a favorite of Madam Captain who had, I suspect, an eye for manly beauty but who appreciated still more a vigor of character that neither cringed nor sulked and that carried on with boldness and good humor. When Baby Face first became eligible for parole, he had been given a hearing and his parole denied, so he had some six years to go when I first met him. However, he had schooled himself to show the world he could take it, and he never gave a sign that he had been hurt.

We had a new janitor in J-2, a long, loose-jointed fellow with a stooped and shambling walk. He had a great nose and shifty eyes flanked by wide-spread ears. An old hand at prison life, he had been in and out of prison for some eighteen years and he knew how to take it soft. Among population it was an accepted fact that he would inform promptly on his fellow inmates for his own good, and this reputation earned him the nickname "the Rat." I got along amiably enough with him at first. I invited him to read my copy of the *New York Times,* which did not arrive until after I had left for pharmacy in the morning. After a while, however, there were days when the paper did not come, and once within the hearing of the janitor I asked the guard whether he could find out the cause of the trouble. Then I went to my cell. When I turned I saw the janitor standing in the doorway, his face transfigured with venomous hate. At the time I did not understand his actions, but I learned afterward that he had been bartering my paper for cigarettes and thought I was informing on him. He started to abuse me in a torrent of vile language. His face grew mottled, and in his intensity he frothed at the mouth. I looked at him fascinated as if he had been a snake.

Suddenly he swung at me and struck the side of my face. I must have parried the blow partly, for I was not hurt, but I was worried about what he would do next. Then all at once he was pulled backward through the door of my cell with such violence that he sat down sharply in the middle of the corridor. Baby Face was standing over him giving him a tongue-lashing with all his former vileness. I was afraid he might do the fellow some injury and get himself into trouble, so I tried to quiet him. He dragged the janitor to his feet, gave him a violent shove toward the entrance to the cell block, and told him to keep going and that if he caught him bothering me again he'd wring his neck. The janitor kept going. In a few minutes my rescuer calmed down. He turned to me and said, "Reverend, you told me to use those words only when I needed them, and I sure had need of them just now."

The next day, during my rest period in the cell, Dago Blackie visited me on a pass. He brought a box of cigars which he wanted to give me in appreciation of the treatment I gave him in the hospital. As a rule I never accepted favors, but one did not argue much with Blackie whether he offered to give or to take. He told me that population knew of my affair with the Rat, and he had come to see me about it. He had just seen the Rat himself at the entrance to the cell block, and he told me about their encounter.

"Now get me straight—I didn't lay a finger on him, but I left him crumpled in his chair with the snot running out of his nose. He's an old prison bird and he knows what I mean, but he's cunning. He might just figure out a way of getting even without anyone pinning it on him. I hear you're expecting to move; I advise you to do it."

Blackie's penalties were known to be swift and drastic. He had a contempt for rules as things which control timid people and make it all the easier for a bold man to take what he wants. To the world at large he was a dangerous character and had to be kept under lock and key, but in a different social setting he might have become a popular hero by the daring of his exploits. However, I suspect his life would have been a short one. Some months later, a guard Blackie hated as only he could hate aroused his passion. He struck like lightning, and the guard was knocked out. Blackie was subdued by a swarm of guards, given a hearing, and disciplined. Population said he had drawn extra time and had been swallowed up in Alcatraz.

There were other sound reasons why I should leave J-block besides the janitor's enmity. Our block was at the far end of the corridor from the hospital, and I was subject to emergency calls at any time of the day or night. The cell to which I intended to go was in B-3, next to the hospital. The men who lived in it were long-termers. They were considered dangerous and kept under guard, though later the block was given honor status. I knew many of them, and it seemed to me they had acquired a poise in doing time that made for a restrained tranquility. Several days after my affair with the janitor, I transferred to B-3.

I found that my possessions had accumulated to a point where they made a greater load than a man could carry in one trip, so the young man who served as janitor of J-1 got permission to help me. He was a tall chap, handsome in a large way, who chatted engagingly of social functions and social figures from Baltimore to Boston. By profession he had been a gigolo, with an exclusive clientele. As part of his act he had posed as a captain or a major, and was arrested for wearing the uniform illegally. He told me with a smile that he had undertaken to explain to the court that he neither intended to nor did he deceive anybody—the uniform was as much part of his profession as if he had been an actor on the stage— and that his profession was a perfectly respectable one which filled a social need. But the judge did not like gigolos and gave him two years. I was to see much more of him later, for he became a nurse in the surgical ward.

Neither of us had any time to spare at my cell, so we dropped our bundles and departed, he to his cell block and I to pharmacy. When I came back after work, I found that all of my equipment had been carefully stowed away. Some of my pictures were on top of my locker, my cot was made up, and a shade had been put around the light in the center of my cell to relieve the glare. The Army Tank and the Killer, my new neighbors, had done this for me as evidence of their good will.

There were about thirty-five of us in the block, mostly mature men who went about their daily routine in a deliberate way and kept aloof from population as much as possible. It was considered the best way to get along if you wanted to "keep your nose clean." Inmates who were too friendly were likely to be suspected of making improper advances, or they were likely to become involved in other's affairs. Though I am inclined to be friendly, I learned to walk the length of the corridor looking neither to the right nor to the left, seeing no one and speaking to no one unless specifically spoken to.

Among us were two bankers, one my friend from J-block, the clerk to the assistant warden, who had transferred shortly before I did, and the other the librarian of the medical library which I frequently visited. The second was past sixty. He had a massive jaw and head and carried himself with great dignity. In conversation he chose his words slowly and with care. He was doing twenty years and had been in Lewisburg for more than six, and the outside world had receded from him. He had no children, his wife had never visited him, and their correspondence had long since ceased. He was a forgotten man. I found him a fine, rather well-read fellow, and we discussed many subjects, among them the effect on western Christianity of the Reformation. Since he was a Roman Catholic, we had different views on the subject.

Shortly after I became a resident of B-block, he was called in for a hearing by the parole board at its July session. He was interested in the results of his hearing, of course, but had no burning eagerness to get out. Rather to his surprise, in August he received notice that he had been granted parole. Usually there was a considerable gap between the date of notice and the date of release, but in his case the parole was to take effect within twenty-four hours. He was brought face to face with the outside world so suddenly that he was thrown into a panic. His impassive dignity disappeared and he babbled like a child. He seemed incapable of doing the simplest things necessary for his departure. We had to lead him around and direct him on each mission. He became desperate, visited the warden, and besought him to get his parole deferred, but that was impossible; a decree of parole is final. Once it takes effect the United States Government ceases to provide you with board, lodging, clothes, and service. You are an evicted tenant. So he had to go out. I can imagine him stumbling into the outer world blinking like an owl in daylight.

After he was gone the Manager moved into his end cell, and I took the one adjoining his. Across the corridor from me was the Army Tank, and from his window we could look down on the tower over the entrance gate and see the inside door. The Army Tank would contemplate it and say, "We all pass through that door twice, once when we come in and once when we go out. The space between those two passages is just time, filled with restless bitterness. Already I've done seven years. I wonder if I'll ever pass through that gate again."

The Killer, who lived two cells down the corridor, was doing life. To him time had no meaning at all. He was a great hulk of a man with the mind of a child. He had a Bible which he pored over. I could see him sitting hunched in his chair, the book open on his knees, his great index finger following the lines and his lips forming the words. He would sometimes come to my cell and ask me to explain the meaning of phrases that troubled him, and he put many questions to me about God: his love, his wisdom, and his capacity for forgiveness.

Then he might say, "Why should God want me to be here? Why should he want me to do those things that brought me here? Do you believe I'll be forgiven?" They were awkward questions to answer.

The Killer's original transgression of the law had been swallowed up in the offense he committed when the officers came to arrest him. He must have exploded in a flaming wrath, for two men were killed before he was captured. I suppose he was like that too when he killed the German sailor, but as I saw him he was quiet and easy to get along with. And there was something wistful about him, as if he were puzzled by questions he could not answer. But there were other times when he would sit in his cell, immense, immobile, and brooding. Those who had seen more of prison life than I shook their heads and assured me, "He won't make it. Five years more, maybe less, and he'll need a different kind of cell. He needs watching. If he went mad he could be as dangerous as a bull elephant."

The Manager had for a long time been one of my closer friends. His assignment was that of an administrative clerk, and he had organized the baseball teams as a volunteer activity. He was a quiet efficient fellow about forty years old, and in population he was trusted and popular, even though the task he had taken on was not easy. There was an infinite variety of disputes to settle, any one of which might develop into violence. He balanced the teams, chose the umpire, acted as the court of last resort, and carried on with firmness and a minimum of words. Of course, the Killer was behind him, but he never needed protection.

He got a certain satisfaction out of holding a position of importance and inspiring improvements for stockade, but the underlying purpose of it all was securing parole. In managing the teams he was co-operating with the prison administration by helping maintain order, and he felt sure it would help him with the parole board. He was eager to get out, although the only person that he had any contact with in the outside world was his sister. His parents were dead, and his wife had long since divorced him.

He had been sentenced for holding up a mail truck. The other four members of the gang, including his older brother, had never been caught. The Manager drew a double sentence on the theory that he could reveal, if he chose, his brother's whereabouts. At least that was his interpretation of his twenty-five-year stretch, and the injustice of it—for he did not know where his brother was—never ceased rankling. There is always an element of injustice which each sees in his own case. To one man it may be the conviction itself, to another the length of the sentence, and to a third the fact that he had been picked on to be prosecuted while others equally guilty went unmolested.

A number of months after I had taken up residence in B-3, at the October session of the parole board, the Manager had his hearing. In the long pause between the hearing and notice of the decision he carried himself with outward poise, but he was taut with longing. Finally the answer came: "Parole denied." On the day he got his notice I came from pharmacy for a brief period of rest, looked into his cell, and saw him hunched in his chair with his head in his hands. He made no move or sound when I spoke to him. I guessed his trouble and went in and sat down on the edge of his cot. He knew I was there; and after a while he lifted his head, and I saw that his face was distorted and that, though his eyes were directed at me, they were seeing something else. Then he broke into a torrent of words. He damned the parole board, the government, the officers of the jail, the court that sentenced him, and the God that made them and him.

"And I like a goddamn fool co-operated! I helped make it easy for them. What a fool I was! Now they can laugh at me for a sucker. But I'll show 'em. I'll slip something into that baseball crowd that'll start a fight they'll hear on the outside. They won't be able to keep that one inside the walls. It'll shut every cell and lock every gate. They'll pay for this. God, how they'll pay for it!" And on and on.

I waited until the torrent slowed and faltered and stopped, and he sat there staring at nothing, utterly miserable and dejected. Then I started to talk. I suppose we discussed things for an hour or more. It really was not so difficult to get him straightened out. He was a reasonable fellow and when we were through he was prepared to swallow his bitterness so no one would know of it. I had given him a chance to pour it out and to argue himself back to reason.

His conduct after his disappointment was watched closely by the administration. He carried on as before, which was counted strongly in his favor. I had now become sufficiently accepted by the prison administrators to be asked my opinion about the attitudes toward the jail authorities of inmates I knew; about the Manager I could say truthfully that the denial of his parole had been a bitter disappointment, but that he had recovered his poise and could be trusted.

Not so long after, I saw the Swede go out, and then the Kid, both on "good conduct" terms. They were called upon to sign a pledge of good behavior for the remainder of their sentences. As I well knew, the Kid would sign nothing, but he was gone, and the story went the rounds that the warden had signed for him saying, "I'm his official guardian and sponsor anyway."

My third Christmas in jail, that of 1944, drew near. I stayed in pharmacy until nine o'clock on Christmas Eve, and when I entered the cell block I noticed decorations in the long corridor; at the far end were several tables about which were gathered some twenty men. The tables were also decorated and bore cakes and a pot of hot chocolate (taken, I learned, from the officers' mess while the officers graciously looked the other way). When I came up to the table I was saluted with the greetings of the season, and the Manager asked me if I would say something befitting the occasion. I told them as simply as I could the familiar story of the Nativity and spoke of Christ born as a man who grew up in a world that came to hate and fear him. We too, whether rightly or wrongly, were hated and feared by the outside world. But he did not return hate for hate. He too suffered at the hands of the world, and yet he forgave. If we should ever return to the outside, we should go into it without hate.

Then I told them the story of "Silent Night," of the priest who wrote the words and his reason for writing them, and of his friend the organist who composed the music overnight so he could play it for the priest at morning services. Then we sang "Silent Night"—rather, we intoned it. The quality of our singing may have been dubious, but it had an emotional appeal I shall never forget.

Our guard, disturbed by the unusual sound, appeared at the retaining gate. He was an elderly man, as well liked by the prisoners as guards could expect to be. The Manager spoke to him reassuringly: "It's all right, Papa, we're not planning a jail break."

You may understand why I wrote in my letters to my wife that one could find good souls in prison, men who were better than the outside world thought them to be, and that God might be found there too.

20.

'MOLZAHN IS IN DANGER . . . '

I wrote to my wife once that I lived in two cells, one of tangible prison walls, the other in my mind. The second was peopled with my family and my friends. I was an invisible guest at all their social gatherings and a participant in their activities. I was familiar with some of their troubles and problems, patricularly those of my children, and I could ponder over them and give my advice, which, I suspect, was as effective told to my cell walls as it might have been at home.

How fast the children were changing! My older daughter had been fifteen when I was taken away, and my younger daughter, the baby, was twelve. Two years is a long time at that age. My older daughter's eighteenth birthday would be in June. Her mother, before her own eighteenth birthday, had been called upon to make the most important decision of her life when I asked her to become my wife. Life did not give children much time to prepare for great decisions. Now my daughter was a young lady, and I was troubled by what I read of the doings of the younger generation.

I gave wise advice about living which was well received, at least by my cell walls. I wrote it also. Undoubtedly at home it was given the consideration and respect such advice customarily receives. I expressed the wish that my daughters would not use artificial coloring—their natural color was fine enough. It was wrong to spoil it. I have no doubt that the admonition was received respectfully enough ("Poor father, he's such a dear, but so out of this world"). Similarly I advised my son about his schoolwork and urged him to continue with his Latin, which he found difficult, for Latin is an elemental base in western European languages and its study provides a daily routine and patient progress which form excellent mental discipline. He dutifully kept on with Latin.

The reports of the activities of my three youthful offspring rather bewildered me, and I wrote about "our spirited and lively children," expressing the hope that what had happened to their father would not affect the joy they should be having at this time of their lives when today was but the threshold of a more interesting tomorrow. If I had gone back in my mind to my own youth, I might have felt less apprehensive, for the young cannot keep in mourning for a past catastrophe, however grave and clinging it may be.

My catastrophe had, of course, made a difference in their lives—or at least their way of living. Old Zion had a new pastor by the middle of 1943. My salary ceased, and my family moved from the parsonage to a rented home in the section of Philadelphia known as Germantown. They would have been helpless save for the advice and generosity of friends. I felt distractingly useless, but they made out surprisingly well, and all I could do was to write my appreciation: "Friends in need are messengers from God. They show that God has ways and means of expressing his loving-kindness to his children through other human hearts." No matter how I might try, I can never express my full appreciation of those who stood by us with such devotion and loyalty through all our trouble, at a time too when to do so excited the inquiry and suspicion of the agents of the Department of Justice.

"On Sunday morning," I wrote, "when there is a quiet time, I follow the sacred routine which directed our life for many years." In my mind I could place myself in my church, and

216

I continued to do so even after it became official that I was no longer its pastor. News of Old Zion was always of great interest. There were those whom I had known well who died. There were young men I had known in Sunday school and had confirmed in the church who were killed on faraway battle-fields. For them all I spoke and wrote a benediction.

Naturally my wife's letters and visits served to sustain this inner "cell" of my life. After her visits I held tight to the re-membrance. If my duty called me back to pharmacy, I locked up the memory in a recess of my mind until I could be alone with it again.

My elderly friend, my lawyer from Philadelphia, also visited me a number of times. He still refused to admit that he could not obtain the belated justice of a pardon for me. It always seemed as if he had seen or was about to see the Attorney General or one of his assistants, or that he was preparing a letter reiterating his arguments and citing some new item that seemed persuasive, or that he had interviewed some prominent citizen to secure his active interest in my case. Failures could not stop him. He said that so long as life should last he would never give up the fight, and he meant it. I appreciated what he was doing. It cheered me to know that someone cared about righting what he considered a great wrong, but my faith in the machinery of justice had been too rudely shattered to sustain any hope.

At the convention of the Pennsylvania Ministerium, the synod of which I was a member, in May, 1944, my case came up for consideration. There were those in the group who wished to have me removed from the ministry; also there were those, I am glad to say, who were prepared to fight for me. My lawyers in Philadelphia prepared a brief analysis of my case for the faction defending me. This was printed in leaflet form to be distributed to the delegates. The effort was not needed. The convention did what such bodies often do—avoided the issue by postponing action until I should be in a position to appear and defend myself.

I was pleased, although the proceedings seemed to relate to remote matters now. Some of the leaflets were sent to the Department of Justice and my wife brought one or more copies to the prison. I was not permitted to see them for some time, but apparently the prison officials saw them, for I noticed a change in attitude on the part of some who formerly, without knowing any of the details of my case, had looked upon me as a Nazi spy.

The year 1944 began in prison with an epidemic of influenza lasting a month or more. Every bed in the hospital was occupied, and several cell blocks had to be converted into temporary quarters for the sick. The members of the hospital staff, including the pharmacist, were busy day and night, and we took our rest at such times as we could. Fortunately I was not stricken though I did get a bad cold which held on well into February. I had been losing weight steadily; my left ear, the first world war casualty, became a source of constant suffering, and I grew more conscious of pains in my left chest and arm. These pains had come and gone for quite some time, and I attributed them to something in the nature of muscular cramps. They frequently interfered with my breathing and my sleep.

In August of that year, while at my desk in the drug room, I had one of these muscular spasms and was struggling to breathe when the young doctor from across the way entered the room. He noticed my trouble, promptly threw his arms about me to compress my chest and release it, which he did a number of times until my condition was relieved. He insisted on giving me a thorough examination at once, including a cardiogram, and submitted the report to the Chief. I was gravely warned against overexertion and was given a prescription of phenobarbital pills and Veronal, which afforded relief for some weeks and enabled me to sleep. The weather that summer of '44 was oppressively hot. The concrete walls of the cell block retained the heat of the sun all through the night. I blamed my physical state on the enervating climate, and looked forward to cooler weather when I felt I should recover.

In the latter part of September I was given my annual physical examination, which was checked against my original examination of two years before and that of the previous year. My weight was one hundred and fifty-eight pounds, compared with my normal weight of nearly a hundred and eighty. On the bottom of the report was written, "Molzahn is in danger of acute angina pectoris. Must not lift or carry weighty articles." In official writing this comment seemed starkly ominous.

The Chief notified the administration office, the guards, and the other inmates that these warnings were to be observed, and Madam Captain ordered me to use the elevator in the hospital. Since inmates were normally forbidden to use it, there was a question as to how discrimination in my favor would be received. In population all are equal if not free, and a special privilege for anyone may cause trouble. The elevator operator himself might resent it. Our operator, known as "Buck," was a heavy-set colored fellow serving one of those magnificently liberal army sentences of forty years for rape. He cheerfully accepted his instructions concerning me and seemed pleased to co-operate in making sure that I did not walk up stairs.

However, there was no elevator in the cell blocks, and I had to climb two flights of stairs to reach my cell in B-3. And it was not easy to slow down in my job. The sick call line had to be kept moving, there were emergency calls to help someone often in graver danger than I, and the routine work of pharmacy must go on. My condition did not improve.

My ear also continued to fester and ache. In January a doctor from Lewisburg, to whom troublesome cases of the ears, nose, and throat were referred, examined it and gave me an injection of penicillin. I noticed that he addressed me by name, and before he left he asked, "You don't remember me?" I had to admit that I didn't. Then he told me that he had been a member of the board of Susquehanna University when I was there as a teacher and student. He told me that the people in Selinsgrove had all followed my case with interest, and that not one of those who knew me believed me guilty.

"I'm glad to hear that," I said. "I remember the men I met there with affection, and my stay there was one of the pleasantest episodes of my life. I would hate to have them think I undertook to betray the people I lived and worked with."

When he had gone and I was alone with the young staff doctor, I turned to him and asked bluntly, "Do you think I am guilty?"

He answered without hesitation, "I do not, and what's more, not a member of the staff does."

I thanked him. "That's a great help," I said. "It may not get me out, but it makes my stay here easier."

There came an evening toward the end of February, 1945. I was in the drug room, and the Bone-Breaker was in his clinic, which he preferred during waking hours to his dormitory. An attack, the most violent I had yet experienced, assailed me. The muscles of my chest knotted in a cramp. I gasped for breath. The severe pain in my left side traveled down my left arm, which became numb and useless. I thought if I could lie down I would feel better so I pulled myself out of my chair and got to the Bone-Breaker's office. He helped me stretch out on one of the tables used for his treatments, and with my consent began to work on me. For him everything was curable by chiropractic treatment. I was lying face downward and he was cautiously kneading my back muscles and working on my spine when I began to feel as if I were strangling. I could only gasp, "Get me up." I was incapable of moving myself, and he half-lifted me to a chair where I struggled for air while he stood by helplessly watching me. Slowly the constriction loosened, and I could breathe more freely.

When I could speak I said, "Not a word to a soul, Doctor. This is just between us." According to our unwritten code, we prisoners did not invite the authorities into our private affairs.

Shortly afterward I was again examined on the Chief's orders, and a further cardiogram was taken as a check on my previous one. The report was not reassuring. In my next letter home I wrote, "God sends us every so often a friendly warning that this troublesome earth is not our permanent home." Nitroglycerine tablets were prescribed, and on April 8 I wrote to my wife, "For your own peace of mind the tablets I am taking are not dangerous. I have the doctor's assurance of this. I take them three or four times daily and they ease the pain almost at once." My letter dated April 15, 1945, is the last of my correspondence; it was the date of the anniversary of our engagement. "I look back on those happier days, in all probability the happiest of my life," I wrote. "My inner life is blest with rich memories, blest with the happiness you have given me through the years, so blest that I can at times achieve peace and tranquility and gratitude in this world of misery to which my body has been banned."

On the morning of April 17, after a strenuous hour of attending to sick call, I had another attack and again dragged myself as far as the chiropractor's clinic to stretch out on one of the tables. This time the Bone-Breaker attempted no treatment, and after helping me lie down disappeared. Presently the first surgeon entered the clinic. The chiropractor had obviously violated the code. My visitor felt my pulse; then he too was gone. A few minutes later the Manager came into the room, having inquired for me at the drug room. He was startled at finding me in such condition. My helper John had told him where I was but not what to expect.

I felt that if I could just get to my cot I would soon be all right, so I asked him to help me get there. He was dubious about the proposal, but I pleaded so earnestly that he gave in, assisted me to my feet, and supported me as we made our way out of the hospital. At the top of the first flight of stairs in B-block I could go no further. Fortunately the Army Tank came upon us and helped me reach my cell and lie down on the cot. Once there, I did not risk the extra pain of moving. I closed my eyes and concentrated on breathing and hoping that the pain of the cramp would pass away. When I opened my eyes again, the second surgeon was looking down at me. He was armed with a hypodermic needle, its point buried in sterilized cotton. Behind him was a hospital nurse. The Manager had found them coming out of the chiropractor's clinic, to which they had been sent by the first surgeon. The Manager too had violated the code.

I gasped, "Don't send me to the hospital, I'll be all right soon." The surgeon smiled and said that I could use a little help, then mopped a place on my arm and gave me a shot of morphine. In about ten minutes the injection began to take effect, the knotted tension of the muscles of my chest slowly relaxed, and the pain lessened. Presently it was gone completely. I breathed freely once more, and my body was at ease. Then it began to feel light, as though I could float in the air, and my mind was suffused with a great comfort. I was far above all physical and earthly troubles. It seemed that I could look down upon the world from a secure vantage point.

I was fully conscious that two nurses and my two friends from the cell block put me on a stretcher and carried me downstairs to the main corridor onto a reclining wheel chair; I was pushed into the hospital, taken to the surgical ward on the elevator, and deposited on a cot in a private room. I made no protest. I was superior to mundane things. The doctor gave orders to the nurses that every means should be taken to prevent my vomiting when the effect of morphine wore off.

Some time after his departure, Madam Captain entered the room. She gave brisk orders to the nurse about his duties, and to me she said, "I've been expecting this. You've done plenty for others in this hospital, now you're going to get some of it back."

I said, "I shall be out of the way shortly. I have to go back to pharmacy; there's nobody there and a lot to be done." I was still comfortable, but the cloud I had been riding was settling down onto a firmer base. She told me most emphatically that I was going to stay where I was until I was told to get up and that I was not to move from that bed without the doctor's orders.

I defied her that night when the nurse on duty was not around. I got up and went down the corridor to the toilet. The nurse found me crumpled up unconscious and had to call for help to carry me back to bed. In the morning, informed of my insubordination, Madam Captain reprimanded me harshly. If I wanted to die, that was my business, but I had no right to be selfish about it and put everybody else in the wrong.

I had accumulated a considerable background of medical knowledge in the hospital and had discussed my own condition objectively with the doctors. In a general way, as I understood it, the spasms were caused by an interference with the circulation of the blood in the vicinity of the heart, which affected its action and produced a muscular constriction that confined my breathing and made me gasp desperately for air. Under morphine the condition cleared, but left a cardiac inflammation which could readily result in another attack until the outraged tissues had healed. The basic cause for my condition may have been a cardiac weakness, but this was apparently aggravated by emotional strain. In discussing my condition with me at an earlier period of its development the Chief had remarked soberly, "It's due to your mental condition. If you only blew your top now and then, it might help, but you don't. You swallow your troubles."

In the first week of confinement my condition worsened and was viewed with grave concern. Among others the warden visited me; afterward, as I learned later, he telephoned my lawyers in Philadelphia and recommended that my wife come to see me as promptly as possible. He also passed along the Chief's professional opinion that I would not recover unless taken out of jail.

My wife came the next day. Her presence cheered me, but after she left my mind became inert. It is hard to recall just what I did feel. I realized that I was near death, but I was not much concerned. I did not welcome it, nor did I dread it. I do remember, however, that I would get shivers of emotion and cried readily. In one of my letters I had written that some prisoners laugh all the time to avoid weeping but that I had never had a hearty laugh since I arrived in prison, nor had I ever wept. Now I wept uncontrollably.

My wife told me afterward how shocked she was when she first saw me. I was shrunken like a mummy, and my face was no bigger than a hand. My condition was aggravated by an attack of pleurisy about ten days after confinement, and I had to be strapped in bed to get relief in breathing. I became even more frail.

There was evidence that steps were being taken to secure my release. A parole officer, no friend of mine, appeared with papers to sign. In them was the familiar question, "What was the nature of your crime?" followed by a blank space. I told him I had committed no crime and would not sign. He gruffly told me that it was the warden's orders and my lawyers also urged it, but I still refused. The next day my elderly attorney from Philadelphia came to see me with papers satisfactorily filled out. I signed, but I did not expect anything to come of it.

Most of the time I seemed to have little relation to the world about me. Only the visits of my wife stirred my interest. She came as often as she could, and I learned afterward how gracious everybody was to her, from the guard at the entrance tower to the Chief and the warden himself. Buck, the elevator operator, cheerfully gave her express service to the third floor. She was given the number of the telephone in the Chief's office so she could call him from Philadelphia without going through the prison switchboard. Whenever she called, the Chief would come up and tell me, "Your sweetheart just called up," and then give me some message from her. One day he did not come, so I asked the nurse to go down and find out why. Soon the Chief appeared and explained why my wife had not telephoned; then he said jokingly, "You're an exacting man with your sweetheart; I might suppose you suspected me of running off with her."

In several weeks I was permitted visitors. In fact, the Chief encouraged them to a certain degree to keep me interested in living. The two younger medical and surgical doctors had taken over pharmacy and called frequently to ask quiet questions. I had installed a reasonably thorough system, cataloguing each item and describing each process, so they really had no difficulty; but in jest they chided me for the overtime work I had imposed on them.

Daily I had a visit from some of my friends in B-3. The Manager told me on one of his visits that the warden had suggested he might move to the farm dormitory. This was a build-up for a resubmission of his case to the parole board— a show of confidence of that nature would speak louder than words. The Manager thought it mighty decent of the warden and added, "Maybe I'll get a better deal the next time my case comes up. It's lucky you saved me from blowing my top."

The Army Tank came and talked of his son, and one time he told me he had been given a second hearing by the parole board and was waiting for the answer. His voice was restrained and even, but his eyes smoldered in his granite face, and his great hands gripped his knee in a vice.

At times the Killer blotted out the chair at my bedside with his great bulk and fumbled with embarrassment at odds and ends of conversation intended to convey sympathy and comfort. His hands fidgeted uneasily. The others told me that he was eager to come but relieved when he got away. The Banker came with his expressionless mask of a face and talked of men and things, and there clung to his words a whimsical humor that was indefinable.

The Top Man looked in every other day and in his low mellow voice told me of the goings-on in population and in administration as well. He knew everything, and could give his anecdotes a half-cynical, half-humorous twist so that each represented a facet of his favorite study, mankind. I learned that he had moved from H-2 to I Block, where he had a cell for two. In population his new quarters were rated the deluxe accommodations of the jail. The cell had been specially equipped and furnished by a previous administration for a long-since-departed millionaire.

"There comes a time," the Top Man explained, "when it

226

enhances one's prestige to become somewhat remote from the populace, provided the withdrawal can be made with appropriate dignity. I believe my recessional complied with the formula, and I took my clerk, Blackie, with me."

He was reassuring about my legal case, saying that in his judgment it was ripe for favorable action. I knew he meant what he said, but remained unconvinced. On the days he did not come, he sent Blackie to see me for a firsthand report.

Baby Face, who was nurse on the floor below, slipped in to see me every day. When he came he livened the air with crisp remarks, devoted in part to the latest news of J-block and, on one occasion, an extraordinary bit of information about himself. He had nearly six years to serve yet, but that was all changed. He was going out. When he told me, he seemed more subdued than I had ever known him and explained it in this way:

"You see, I have a mother on the outside. She can't get here often, but she never gave me up, even though everybody else did, and she was determined to get me out. She wouldn't take 'no' for an answer. When the parole board turned her down, she haunted everybody else in Washington until finally they surrendered. My sentence was commuted, so I can go out on 'good conduct' term next week."

He stopped, and I could see him staring at the wall over my head. The news was almost incredible. Presently he said, "I'm glad I cut a lot of the rough stuff out of my talk. She wouldn't like it. I guess she's the only person in the world who thinks I'm worth a damn."

I looked at him and shook my head. "No, there are others," I said.

He got up out of the chair suddenly and with a gruff "goodbye" walked out of the room. He wasn't feeling too tough just then.

Seven weeks passed. My pleurisy cleared up, and there was

no recurrence of angina. My condition improved, but it was still precarious. A new attack might be fatal. I must have been a wreck of a man, for my weight had fallen below one hundred and thirty pounds. From time to time I received news of the application for my release. My wife spoke of it hopefully, and I pretended an interest I did not feel and a faith I did not have.

On Saturday, June 2, the Manager dropped in for a visit and a chat. He told me he had moved out to the farm dormitory, and he was describing life there and his own crude efforts at farming. Suddenly he got up and went out; as he did so, the warden and the Chief entered. The first stood at the foot of my bed and looked down at me. "Can you stand good news, Reverend?" He had never before addressed me as "Reverend."

"I can stand bad news," I replied. He smiled, then told me that he had just received notice by teletype from Washington that the President had signed my commutation of sentence and that I was no longer a prisoner of the United States.

I murmured, "I don't believe it," and looked at the Chief. He nodded. The warden went on. "You are now a problem. You're no longer under my jurisdiction. You don't belong here, and yet here you are. You are now a guest of the United States Public Health Service, and the Chief is your host."

After they were gone, the Manager came back. His eyes were shining with excitement. For the Chief and the warden to visit me together meant something significant. When they came he had slipped into the nurses' office, and the men there were eagerly awaiting the answer. So I told him what the warden had told me and added quietly that I didn't believe it.

"Nonsense!" he said. "It must be true." He walked up and down the room. "Of course it's true," he said, "and if you can get out of this place you'll recover. That's the thing that's been worrying the doctors. They knew you'd never come out of this hospital alive unless you were going out to go home."

I still could not quite comprehend it. Then I asked, "Why did the Chief look at you the way he did when he found you here?"

"He knew I didn't have a pass to come see you. I had a pass to the pharmacy and I just walked upstairs." Then he said thoughtfully, "The Chief won't say anything about it— he's not that kind. But I'd better get back to lawful territory." Before he went downstairs he passed the news on to the nurses.

The Chief came back not long after with Madam Captain. She dabbed my arm with alcohol and the Chief gave me morphine. "I'm not excited," I told him.

"Just a precaution," he replied. "We must get you out of here safely, you know. Your attorneys in Philadelphia will be notified from Washington, and your wife should be up here promptly to take you away. We regret that we can't provide an ambulance to take you home."

As they were leaving, Madam Captain looked down at me and said, "So you're leaving us. Well, well, well!" Then she chuckled—and I am sure the count was four. By now the realization that I was going out was beginning to take hold, and the Chief's precaution was justified.

My wife came to see me the next morning, Sunday. She had left Philadelphia the previous afternoon too early to get the news. She came to the penitentiary early and was puzzled by the cheery reception she got from the guards, who spoke of the good news. At first she thought this must mean a miraculous turn for the better in my condition. When she entered my room I asked about the ambulance. This troubled her, and when I babbled about going home that day she was convinced that my mind was affected. As soon as she could, she slipped out of the room. Downstairs she met the guard, who confirmed what I had said and who opened the Chief's office so she could telephone him at his home and get an authoritative version of the story and instructions as to what should be done next.

When she returned to me, her visit became a thrilling one, and when she left to make arrangements for an ambulance and hospital accommodations I was alight with anticipation. The incredible had happened: I was really going home.

Population buzzed with interest. A commutation terminating a sentence did not happen every day. The Top Man came himself and inquired particularly about the names of my lawyers. I could readily imagine the nature of the discussions in population of how the release had been achieved; I could see the foxier inmates hinting at mysterious influences and their hints like winged creatures flying busily about the walled-in space. Some inmates, I am sure, were sincerely pleased at my good fortune, but to many the vital interest lay in commutation as a possible solution to their own problems.

It was not a simple matter at that time to get an ambulance for a full day's duty. Monday came and with it a report that no ambulance was yet available, but late in the day we heard that one could be expected the following morning. At midday on Tuesday I was told that it had arrived and that my wife had come with it and was waiting for me at the entrance tower.

There were many details to be taken care of before I could depart. My possessions were packed by my friends in B-3. Ordinarily there was a careful segregation of what might and what might not be taken out, but this rule was waived. However, there was one official requirement I could not escape. Outgoing prisoners must be clothed and shod. I insisted I was traveling in pajamas, but there was no escape. My legs were thrust into a pair of pants, a jacket was put about my shoulders, shoes on my feet, and the rest of my gear tucked in a bundle beside me. I distributed certain minor possessions among my friends—a few toilet articles, a tobacco pouch, a pair of shoes, and finally the wrist watch I had bought in the commissary for two dollars and fifty cents. This I gave to the Gigolo. He had nursed me faithfully.

At last I was on my way. I reached the first floor on a wheeled stretcher and was kept waiting there while further plans were debated for the better part of an hour. During this time many men circled about me, some of them coming up to say goodbye, others talking freely over me; I heard an argument between a guard and an administrative officer, each of whom asserted that he was the appropriate person to go with me to Philadelphia. A trip to the city offered a welcome break in the routine of their lives.

Apparently the delay arose from the fact that a decision had to be secured from some high authority on whether I should be wheeled to the ambulance at the entrance gate or the ambulance should be brought through the rear gate to the hospital. Finally the decision was made. The Chief came out of his office accompanied by the young staff doctor and Madam Captain. The ambulance was to come to the hospital, and the staff doctor was to go with me to Philadelphia. I was given an injection of morphine and wheeled into the elevator. My last recollection of the hospital is of Madam Captain standing at the head of my stretcher while the injection was given; her hand stroked my hair, and I heard her say, "You'll make it. You must. Goodbye, and thanks for all you've done." It was something to puzzle over and cherish.

I was lowered to the basement and carried up the steps which for all of us once had led down to the receiving room. As the ambulance drove away, I could see a scattering of blue-clad men in stockade gazing after us, and others as we drove past the industries building and the coal pile. They all waved, and I can imagine the longing to be with me that gripped them. They stared after us until the ponderous gate rolled across the exit. Now we were outside the main wall but still within the containing wall, where we remained until the ambulance had been searched for stowaways. Then the second gate opened, we drove outside and around the jail to the front gate; it opened, and my wife and our friend emerged with the warden and the Chief, both of whom stood by until we were ready to drive off. As a parting word of advice the Chief said, "With care and the urge to live he can make it." Then with a bow to my wife he added, "I'm sure he'll have both."

In a moment more we were gone, and the Pen at Lewisburg was no longer a reality in my life. It had taken its place in my memory as a horrid nightmare. For years afterward it was to haunt my dreams, from which I would awake with a start, thinking I was still encased in concrete and steel. My waking moments, too, it haunted. For a long time I felt a compelling urge to talk about the prison and the men in it to anyone who would listen.

21.

'MINISTER OF THE CHURCH'

Perhaps I should tell you what happens to a man who re-enters life at fifty with a damaged heart and with a cloud of widespread suspicion and disapproval hanging over him. Before I left the penitentiary at Lewisburg, little of my reputation as a Nazi spy still clung to me. I was accepted or rejected by staff members and inmates on my own merits, but I soon found that the outside world had its own ideas about me and held on to them tenaciously.

It was late in the afternoon when we drove up to the hospital where we presumed a room had been reserved and would be available on my arrival. The white-uniformed staff doctor got out of the ambulance and entered the hospital to make necessary arrangements. It shouldn't have taken long, but time passed and he didn't return. Then, well over an hour later, he came back in a state of great indignation. He was accompanied by orderlies, who carried me in and deposited me in makeshift quarters behind a screen in a hallway. The doctor said nothing to me in explanation, but I heard him give full and explicit instructions concerning my treatment to an unresponsive intern. Then he wished me a good recovery and departed.

He told my wife what had happened, however. When he reported my arrival at the admissions desk he was informed coldly that the hospital had no room for me and I must be taken elsewhere. He was much surprised and soon much irritated. He insisted curtly that the answer given would not do. He was there as a representative of the Government of the United States, under its orders to deliver me to that particular hospital. Ample advance notice of my coming had been given, and I would have to be received. His attitude was so disturbing that he was referred to higher authority. Finally a superior official grudgingly directed that I be provided for.

I remained in the hallway several days while controversy raged in the building, and at length I was admitted to a room. The intern who gave me injections did so with a spitefulness that indicated a preference for sticking the needle through my heart. It was a re-enactment of my early days in the prison.

Others, however, felt differently about me. Somehow many knew of my coming to the hospital, and a number of letters arrived expressing good will, together with a quantity of flowers so great that my room could not accommodate them all. Clearly I was still something of a symbol of political and perhaps religious significance which gave rise to widely different reactions. But days passed, and the newspapers made no reference to my release. We fondly hoped that I had faded from the popular mind and no longer had news value, but we were shortly undeceived.

A week after my arrival at the hospital a Philadelphia afternoon paper carried a story with the heading:

REVEREND KURT MOLZAHN FREED ON ORDERS OF PRESIDENT
Minister of Old Zion Here
Was Convicted as Nazi Spy in 1942

My case was interwoven with the recent release of the Princess Hohenlohe from internment and the decision of the United States Supreme Court handed down the day before setting aside the conviction of some twenty-three Bundists for

234

obstructing the draft. The morning newspapers played up my story the next day. One snappy headline read:

MOLZAHN, GERMAN SPY, RELEASED BY TRUMAN

Heated editorial comment linked the Supreme Court's decision and my case as proof that we were getting soft on Nazis although the surrender of the German Army was only a month old. The matter continued to attract attention over a period of a month and gave rise to some lively "letters to the editor," most of them antagonistic towards me, though a few vigorously supported me.

Much of this controversy was kept from me at the time, but I knew it was going on and was unavoidably affected. Such news stories probably arouse only casual interest in many readers, but for those directly affected they blot out all else in the paper and are a cause of great discomfort. However, we lived through it. On the day the story broke, I sat up for the first time in eight weeks, and two days later I was discharged from the hospital and driven home. The management of the hospital was probably as gratified at my departure as I was at departing.

Our new home was not a gracious place like Old Zion parsonage. It was characterless, too old to be convenient and not old enough to have acquired charm. But as I had written from jail, "Home is where a loving heart is waiting for you," and at last I was home. I was determined to get well. I had so much to live for—Nini, the children, the many friends who wrote their well wishes and who came to visit me in person to express them. Of the more than eight hundred letters I received, only one snarled at me for being a wicked Nazi. I was resolved also to come back. I might be beaten down, but I was not going to stay down.

My recovery continued satisfactorily. In less than two weeks

I could go about the house with the aid of a cane. In six weeks I could take short walks outside and had filled out sufficiently to look like myself again. However, I was still under strict orders from my doctor to be extremely careful in my movements. With the improvement in my physical condition, I suspect I became impatient. I had much to be thankful for, but I wanted to be doing something. I tried to write of life in prison, the memory of which was vivid, and I was bothered with the belief that my powers of concentration had been destroyed and that I could no longer write or think consecutively. What I succeeded in putting down seemed to have no relation to reality.

I turned over in my mind all possible ways of making myself useful. I could not function as a minister unless my suspension was revoked, and before that could be done a hearing must be held by the Committee on Discipline. Then its recommendation must be acted upon by the Ministerium convention, which would not occur until the following May. Any occupation calling for physical effort was out of the question for me, and I speculated on the possibility of teaching Latin, Greek, or Hebrew. When I inquired about openings, there were none—those languages were apparently out of fashion. I protested rather ungraciously that there were intangible walls in the outside world that shut a man in like the stone walls of a prison.

I had to content myself with reading, walking, listening to the radio and doing such minor work as I could about our new home. We had been obliged to leave the first house when it changed ownership soon after my return, and so, with the help of generous friends, we bought a place. During this period I had occasional reminders that my heart was none too strong, and in the latter part of December, 1945, when I rashly undertook to shovel snow from the sidewalk, I had an attack of such gravity that I was taken to the hospital and put under an oxygen tent for some weeks.

While I was in the hospital the Committee on Discipline heard my case. The question before it was whether I had conducted myself in a manner incompatible with the ministry. At the hearing I was represented by devoted adherents, but there was also a bitterly antagonistic opposition. The committee, of course, could not conduct a new trial, but as an independent tribunal it had to decide whether the court record showed that I had done anything incompatible with my duties as a minister. The evidence of that could be found only in the priest's conversation with me. The committee recommended my reinstatement. In May at the convention of the Ministerium at Buck Hill Falls, Pennsylvania, this recommendation was adopted by a vote of 481 to 56:

> 1. We recommend that the Ministerium of Pennsylvania concur in the decision of the Committee on Discipline and find Mr. Molzahn not guilty of "conduct incompatible with the character of the ministerial office."
> 2. We recommend that the suspension which was properly imposed upon him be now lifted and his name continued on the roll of the Ministerium.
> 3. We further recommend that the President of the Synod should in his pastoral capacity admonish Mr. Molzahn and all other members of the Ministerial Session to the end that no one may in the future find himself in the position where charges may be brought against him either in the name of the Church or of the State.

In its "Findings" the committee made this statement:

> It is to be admitted that ordinarily, when a minister has been found guilty of criminal misconduct by the courts of the land, it is a legitimate conclusion . . . that he must have been guilty of "conduct incompatible with the character of the ministerial office."

In spite of this, the Committee on Discipline finds itself unable in the present instance to point to any intentional or deliberate act or attitude on the part of Mr. Molzahn which it can properly term "conduct incompatible with the character of the ministerial office." This conclusion rests upon our study of the original transcript of record from the courts of the United States before which Mr. Molzahn's trial was conducted and his subsequent appeals heard, upon our evaluation of the testimony presented at this trial, and upon the study of the transcript of our hearing in which all the relevant testimony adduced by either the Committee on Investigation or the defense is fully set forth. The Committee on Discipline therefore finds the charges against Mr. Kurt Emil Bruno Molzahn not proved and finds the accused not guilty. . . .

I was still considered newsworthy at that time. The newspapers drew attention to the fact that I, who had been convicted as a Nazi spy, had been reinstated in the ministry; letters written to the press gave voice to outraged feelings that the Lutherans should have so countenanced me.

I was now officially eligible to function as a minister again, but had yet to re-enter a pulpit. What would be my reception if I did conduct church services? The matter was put to the test shortly, for I was invited to officiate and deliver a sermon at Holy Cross Church in Philadelphia. It is a church of substantial size, but one whose congregation had dwindled with the shift of population. No publicity was given to my advent except in the church news letter of limited circulation, but on the appointed Sunday the church, which accommodated seven hundred and fifty people, was filled to capacity with a quiet, undemonstrative congregation. It was a great comfort to me. Some no doubt came out of curiosity, but I could sense a deep feeling of sympathy and faith that filled me with appreciation.

Once the ice was broken, I had similar invitations from other churches and similar receptions. Nevertheless, there was hesitancy about inviting me to take a pastorate, although several churches toyed with the idea. Months passed, and the president of the Ministerium counseled that I be prepared to go to a church in the West or in Canada where my story might not be known. I suppose I did present an uncomfortable problem to one upon whom rested the responsibility for all the churches in our district, but I would not consider the proposal. Philadelphia had been our home too long; it was in fact the only home our children remembered. And even if I had consented, Nini would have vetoed the proposal for reasons I thought were sound. In Philadelphia, where we were known, those who believed in us asked for no explanation. Those who did not would listen to none. The story was bound to follow me wherever we went and divide our society again. No one could forecast its division. It was better to live with those who knew everything about us and were undismayed.

A partial solution to the dilemma came in the fall of 1946 when I was invited to become associate pastor of Holy Cross Church. On Sunday, November 24, I was installed. The news got around, and there was some fear that an effort might be made to interrupt the proceedings. A special police guard was asked for and received, but there were no untoward incidents. Any uncertainty about my reception at Holy Cross was also soon dispelled. The congregation began gathering an hour before the service, and at the appointed time every pew was occupied and the aisles were filled with chairs. I suspect the old church had never seen the like of it.

However, I had to face a resurgence of my old character, for I was greeted with this heading in the newspaper:

REV. KURT MOLZAHN, ONCE JAILED AS NAZI SPY, GETS A NEW PASTORATE FROM THE LUTHERANS

My installation even drew the attention of a well-known radio commentator, who remarked that my case was one of the reasons why the blindfolded lady "Justice" wept. My ten-year sentence for espionage had been commuted on a doctor's certificate that I was dying of a fatal illness. He commented, "And so the convict served only thirty-six months. He got out in June, 1945. A sad ending? Of course not. Last month at a rally of one of those 1000 per cent outfits in Philadelphia, it was announced that Molzahn had just been installed as an associate pastor of the Holy Cross Evangelical Church at Philadelphia. Hallelujah! Nein? Ja!"

I like to think that I have heard the last of that sort of thing, for in January, 1949, I was installed as pastor in my own church, and the news item it evoked was comfortingly brief: "Reverend K. E. B. Molzahn has been called to the pastorate of St. Thomas' Lutheran Church, Herman and Morton Streets, Germantown." Perhaps I am now accepted or rejected solely on my merits as a minister of the church.

It might be asked why, when I was casting around for a place to fill, I did not offer myself as an expert on penology and take to lecturing. Ex-convicts have been known to do very well in that field, but my imagination did not run that way. To lecture, one should have a program to sell that sounds like a solution to a problem. I had no program and no solution. I have written about prison life, not as a problem in sociology, but as the multiple stories of men at odds with society who live encased in steel and concrete. Hundreds more than I have mentioned occupy my memory and are brought into the field of my thoughts by some circumstance that recalls them. Each typified some phase of human emotion manifested in response to the environment, but I am quite unable to find a pattern into which they could all fit.

Maybe I could have made a stir by attacking the administration of the jail. Many things went on there that were not supposed to—guards grafting on rich prisoners, rich prisoners getting favors from guards, and so forth—but any such attack would be out of focus. There was an administrative staff of two hundred and fifty men mingling with fifteen to seventeen hundred inmates. The staff had its share of human failings and wrong judgments, but overall the jail was conscientiously administered.

I might have built up a sensational talk on sex manifestations in prison. They were a recognized element in our life, but this is not a subject I would care to talk about particularly, for I know no answer. Our psychiatrist did not share my reluctance. He talked about it freely and lectured on the subject in the prison to substantial audiences. I think he was rather proud of the attendance he attracted. I expostulated with him that the men were already overcharged with sex urges and that his lectures merely excited them further, but he was not disturbed. He assured me that I was concerned over something far more normal than I suspected; he said it would be a good thing if the administration recognized it instead of attempting suppression. He may be right, but I would rather he wrote about it than I.

There is, I suppose, some confusion in the public mind about the function of a prison. We want to punish offenders, we want to hold them while we rehabilitate them, and we want to protect society against its dangerous members. For all these three purposes we have one answer—prison—and we try to make it fit the varying requirements of each purpose. Prisons may be criticized for not being brutal enough for punishment, or sufficiently well equipped for rehabilitation, or for not being tight enough to hold permanently those feared by society. There can be a point in all three criticisms. I shall attempt no answer, but I can assure those who ask for greater severity that even a well conducted jail provides grave punishment, even though it may not appear in the form of physical brutality.

As I have indicated before, I am not a reformer and have no wish to press society into a common mold for its own good. I am simply a minister of the church whose message of faith and hope I try to deliver and whose congregation I try to know as individuals and tend the way a pastor should.

It has been forty years and more since at the age of fourteen I resolved to go to the United States to carry on the work of the church there. I am where I chose to be, and I never saw myself in any other setting. My place in the church may be less imposing than it once was, my sphere of influence reduced, and my place in the society of my city less prominent, but when one has a race to run it is unwise to glance backward. It throws one out of stride.

I can only repeat the affirmation with which I began: "All things work together for good to them that love God."

A POSTSCRIPT

POSTSCRIPT

A POSTSCRIPT

The days about which I have written are receding into the past. Today I am pastor of the oldest Lutheran church in Philadelphia, with which my own little congregation merged several years ago. Located in the Germantown section of Philadelphia, its rich tradition goes all the way back to 1728. Among the members of my congregation I find officers and other leading men of the synod to which my congregation belongs.

I add this note to the chronicle of my imprisonment from a relatively distant perspective because I feel that the reader of my story will be interested in knowing my present outlook on life.

I am profoundly grateful in view of all that has happened to me and my family that God has guided us so graciously through storm and gloom, and has been with us so tangibly in good and evil days. Even more important, I feel he has kept my heart free from bitterness and resentfulness; my mind still cries out against what I consider an undeserved injustice, but my heart knows that its faith in God and Christ, and even its love for this country, have been deepened by the years of trial.

I can point to many things that have enriched my life as a result of my prison experiences. There are some former inmates with whom I still have contact, men who shared my lonely days at Lewisburg and became my friends. One former inmate who helped write a petition for my release is now an immediate neighbor. In the company of the man I call "Army

Tank" I attended the ordination of his son into the ministry. It was a fulfilment of prayers we offered together during our confinement.

The sympathetic hearts of some of the guards who had charge of me during those years shall not be forgotten. One wrote to me after my release, "Never will I forget how you made it possible for me to eat my meals in peace while at the prison hospital post, where you had charge of the drug room, etcetera. . . . You will remember that I always had faith in you, and that I did my best to give you all the encouragement possible when things looked so very dark for you, my friend."

Nothing I could say would show my true feelings toward all the people who stood by me and my family throughout all the years of our distress—members of my congregation, friends from all walks of life, and especially an "inner circle" of those who were intimate friends of the family. They all came to my defense and to the aid of my wife and children when to do so was to cast suspicion on themselves. I know they do not wish to be mentioned by name here, but I must mention my spiritual adviser, the Rev. Dr. Paul Hoh. While he was president of the Lutheran Theological Seminary in Philadelphia, this distinguished theologian and church leader visited me often and wrote me many letters. In one, written while my case was being considered by the synod, he said: "I shall do what I can on your behalf. From the very beginning I have believed you to be innocent, and I still believe you to be so. Had I thought otherwise, I should willingly have served on the jury to find you guilty. I would not have lifted a little finger for you, had I for a moment doubted you. It is because I have had implicit faith in your integrity that I was willing to testify as I did on your behalf."

A few years ago Paul died, prematurely but after a rich life.

As his hour of departure drew near, we were alone for a few moments in the hospital room. I thanked him once more for his friendship, for his courageous stand as a witness in my trial, for his kindness, and for the faith he had in me. He said, "Kurt, looking over the years of my life and my ministry, I think I would change many things—would do almost everything in a different way. But one thing I would do again— I would study theology and become a minister to serve my Lord and Master. And so would you, Kurt." A few hours later his warm and loving heart ceased to beat.

I must also express my deepest gratitude to my legal defenders, especially Francis Fisher Kane and T. Henry Walnut. These two men were much more than "my lawyers"; they took my case believing in my innocence, and a deep friendship grew between us and our families. "Uncle Frank," as I came to know Mr. Kane, is no longer with us, after a long and fruitful life. A colleague once called him "an ardent believer in social equality and justice, who championed unpopular causes involving civil liberties and equality before the law and rights of minorities."

It would give the wrong impression if I were to suggest that only these glowing friendships remain of my memories of our time of hardship. There is no way to erase the past. I think I have honestly revealed in the foregoing pages how the whole affair hurt and frightened me at the time. But now that I have reached a summit of the years from which there is only descent, I can indeed see that "The things o'er which we grieved with lashes wet will flash before us out of life's dark night, As stars shine most in deepest tints of blue."

I have not written this book as any sort of self-vindication, as any sort of attempt to justify myself before men. I feel that I have had experiences which should be of interest to a great many people, especially those experiences which deal with prison life. I have tried to be as objective as possible in describing people and things.

Therefore, those who looked within these pages for a burning statement of my innocence followed by a legal brief in its support have probably been disappointed. So too, probably, have those who expected here the "confessions" of a "former Nazi." In the chapter on my trial I have attempted to show accurately the legal nature of the case brought against me, as well as my defense. I could protest once more my innocence, but this I have done all along, and one more protestation is not likely to change anyone's mind.

After I received a commutation of sentence from President Truman my lawyers were determined that the matter should not end there. Mr. Walnut worked unceasingly to obtain a full pardon, which he assured me was the most the government could provide in a case of this sort. At first I was not enthusiastic, for to receive a pardon seemed to imply an admission of guilt, but I began to see that it would also make my dealings with the people around me much easier. Such a pardon, signed by the President, would, I was told, signify that the highest official in the land had accepted me as a proper and loyal citizen as fully and completely as if I had never been accused of an offense against the United States. On this basis the prospect of a pardon became appealing to me, and I cooperated fully in working for it. In 1956 I received a telegram which read, "Full and unconditional pardon granted you by President Eisenhower."

This was the final word in the "Molzahn case." I was happy to receive it, though by this time the whole affair had pretty much passed out of public consciousness. I was able to carry on my affairs without bearing the burden of the past; at first I was fearful that the pardon would stir up another controversy, but to my relief the newspapers took no note of it. It goes without saying, then, that I believe firmly that the publication of this book will not stir up any dead issues.

I have told you who I am, what I did, and what I have experienced. If any choose to make something more of the book than this, it is his privilege, but it is also outside the scope of my intentions.

The world has changed since the events described in this book took place. Political, social, and geographical structures have been transformed in the years since the second world war. The place where I was born is no longer a part of Germany; it lies behind the Iron Curtain. The Germany I knew and loved no longer exists. I knew that already in the 1930's when I visited the land of my birth. It became even more clear to me during the two trips I have made there since I was released from prison.

There has been more than just this recognition, however. When I arrived at Susquehanna University in 1924 I had already decided that my life's work and mission was to be in America. From that decision I have never wavered. On my trips to Germany I have revelled in the beauty of the land— the dreaming villages, the towns, the mountains, the meadows, the fields, and the forests—and I rejoiced to hear the mother tongue of my childhood and all the dialects I knew. And yet a strange feeling filled my nostalgic heart. What was it? Not only had Germany changed, but *I* had changed; I discovered that I was a stranger in the land of my birth, and I felt homesick for America, for my work and my congregation, for the way of life my family and I were leading in Pennsylvania.

During the troubled times leading up to the last war I was sick at heart because of the growing hostilities between Germany and the land of my adoption. Nevertheless, I always knew that my ultimate loyalty lay with the United States, and I became a citizen with this firm conviction in mind. Before the war there was a great deal of pro-Nazi sentiment in this country, much of it naturally among German-Americans; in addition there was strong anti-Nazi feeling, which just as naturally was directed at the German-Americans. Through all this storm and dissension I tried to maintain a neutral position. This was not an easy thing to do. Perhaps I was mistaken in taking such a position, and there were probably times when my tactics were wrong; nevertheless, to the best of my knowledge I neither said nor did anything which was disloyal to the United States.

I have come across a notation in my diary dated May 22, 1924: "Today I was ordained and set apart as a minister of the church of Christ. While kneeling in the sanctuary I prayed for God's grace upon my future life and mission in America." As I think back on all that has happened, it seems almost too good to be true that my dream, my life's ambition, is still being fulfilled. I am what I felt I was called to be, a servant of God and his church in America.

And if I am ever tempted to be bitter about my trial and imprisonment, I recall the calm assurance that my friend Paul Hoh gave me in his talks and his letters: "I have very high regard for the courts of our land; no one could have a higher regard for them than I have. I have sat in them hundreds of times, and have served on the jury. Occasionally even our best courts err. That is hardly to be avoided, since even the best of men are sometimes misled, being fallible. I believe an error was made in your case. . . .

"Many years ago one of the most famous and skilful surgeons in America performed an operation on me. He made a mistake during that operation, and that mistake will cost me, I am told, from ten to fifteen years of my life. All together that surgeon performed over 50,000 operations, almost all of them successful. But he did make a mistake at least once in his career. I do not hold it against him. In fact, I would have gone back to him again, had I needed another operation. So it is with our courts. They handle thousands of cases—and I have watched many hundreds of them in my day. Mostly justice is meted out. Once in a while there is a blunder. It is hard on the person who suffers, but I suppose there is as little that can be done about it as there is when a surgeon's knife accidentally slips.

"The important thing, finally, is not so much what happens to us, as the way we take that which happens to us. Our tragic experiences can be stumbling blocks or they can be stepping-stones. Ultimately your experience can lead to a service for our Lord Jesus Christ, greater than you have dreamed of. . . . So, take courage, my friend; 'who treads upon his woes stands higher.'

"This letter is beginning to sound preachy, and I certainly do not want to write you a sermon. For I know that it is not necessary that I write you in this way. You have the spiritual stuff in you to rise above your present experiences, and eventually to conquer them, to make them serve you. And then, there is always God—'nearer than breathing, nearer than hands and feet.' He will keep you, and 'your sorrow shall be turned to joy.' Kurt, keep close to Him who will always be close to you."

Following such advice as this, how could I ever be bitter?

November, 1960   KURT MOLZAHN

Type used in this book
Body, 10 on 12 and 9 on 10 Times Roman
Display, Tempo
Paper: White Standard Antique "R"